GREAT BRAND STORIES

BRAND IT LIKE BECKHAM
THE STORY OF HOW BRAND BECKHAM WAS BUILT

ANDY MILLIGAN

 CYANBOOKS

Copyright © 2004 Andy Milligan

First published in Great Britain in 2004 by

Cyan Communications Limited
61 Cooper Close, London SE1 7QU
www.cyanbooks.com

The right of Andy Milligan to be identified
as the author of this work has been asserted
by him in accordance with the Copyright,
Designs and Patents Act 1988.

A CIP record for this book is available
from the British Library

ISBN 0-9542829-5-7

Printed and bound in Great Britain

This book is dedicated with deepest love and eternal gratitude to the memory of my parents, John and Evelyn; without them the wonderful things that have happened in my life would never have happened.

CONTENTS

ACKNOWLEDGMENTS

I have many people to thank for this book.

First of all, my friends who helped with much of the research: Boh Sang Chin, who showed a Beckham-like dedication to getting original and desk research together; Angela Yeo, who must be one of the speediest as well as the smartest desk researchers around, was unfailing and detailed in her discovery of key facts and figures, and has become a much valued friend; and Sara Tang, my close friend and colleague, who offered insight and advice on putting the book together.

Next, Martin Liu, Pom Somkabcharti and Linette Tye at Cyan who were extremely supportive and patient as deadlines came and went without a manuscript and whose careful and challenging editing was excellent.

And John Simmons, a man for whom I have an enormous admiration and who was foolish enough to give me the opportunity to write this book.

Many others gave me information and ideas, and I am particularly indebted to Nic Couchman and his colleagues at Couchman Harrington Associates for much of the technical information in chapter 8.

And most of all, I am deeply grateful to my loving wife Susannah and our children, Ted and Frank, who had to endure weekends and holidays where a distracted dad buried his head in a computer rather than playing, washing up, doing the shopping or any of the other tasks I should have helped with. Their support and patience were wonderful.

Finally, a big thank you to the man who is the inspiration for this book. Thank you, David, for giving me some wonderful moments of football, and thank you in particular for *that* penalty against *that* team on *that* night in Sapporo in 2002. That was a moment that will live with me for ever.

To all of the above, this book is respectfully dedicated.

PREFACE

For many people the notion of David Beckham as a brand will be a strange one. It will perhaps seem strangest to many of those people who admire Beckham most – people who pay large sums of money to watch him play on a football field. David Beckham is a footballer, and that remains the most important aspect of him. If he were not a footballer of great talent, this book would never have been written.

But there is already much more to Beckham than "footballer." His face on a cover can sell copies of a style magazine; his endorsement will sell anything from football boots to hair products; his presence in a place will arouse enormous interest among people of any age, race or gender. He is a commercial property, and his image is carefully managed by a team of people who are committed to making him one of the world's most valuable individuals.

Brand it like Beckham analyses David Beckham as a brand. As with any brand, the product is absolutely crucial. Until now the product has been "footballer," and the product quality has been high. We can expect this to continue for the next few years. As long as Beckham keeps performing on the pitch – whether for England or Real Madrid or any future team – the core of the brand will remain strong.

What sells, however, is not just Beckham's footballing skills, but the positive qualities that we have come to associate with David Beckham – or Becks, or DB, or 23, or any of the other elements of identity that have become part of the brand. In marketing terms, Beckham is a brand with a purpose, core values and an identity, all of which have been thought about and refined to achieve the maximum commercial effect. This might be because the window of opportunity – a footballer's playing career – is so small, or because this brand might have a life beyond that period. If so, what will the brand become?

No one has looked in detail at Beckham the brand before. When we first started planning the *Great brand stories* series, we decided that one of our aims was to create a better understanding of what makes a brand. Not many years ago, we thought of brands only as consumer goods that you could buy in packets from supermarkets. Now we're beginning to be more comfortable with the idea that companies, charities, services, people and countries can be brands too. Any of these can become more commercially successful if we apply the principles of branding to them.

We asked Andy Milligan to write this book because he combines deep and practical experience of branding with a lifelong love of football. Andy led the Interbrand team that created the visual identity for the 2002 FIFA World Cup. He now heads the Interbrand office in Singapore. His location in South East Asia, where the Beckham brand is a growing phenomenon, reinforces his credentials to write this book.

Through classic branding analysis, Andy dissects the Beckham brand. In doing so he provides insights for fans of David Beckham, but also for anyone interested in the way that brands really work. Those lessons can be applied to brands that you might have imagined were playing a different game altogether. They're not. That's what makes this such a valuable and enlightening book.

John Simmons
Series editor, *Great brand stories*

INTRODUCTION

This is a story about a brand called David. Well, not really a story; more of an analysis, I suppose. Is David Beckham a brand? If so, how has that brand been built? What can we expect of it in the future?

But there is a story here too, the story of a new breed of sports professional: a dedicated athlete on the pitch and a self-marketing brand off the pitch. One who is as comfortable with the paraphernalia of marketing, fashion and media as he is with training grounds, team strips and playing surfaces. One who knows what a pitch is in the football sense *and* the marketing sense.

It is also the story of a unique individual who has held on to and consistently demonstrated his personal beliefs and values in an over-exposed and sometimes incredibly hostile arena. Someone who has been able to balance his passion for football with a flair for fashion. And someone who has emerged at the right time in the right place: when football has become a mass-consumption product available globally 24 hours a day through every means of modern communication from digital TV to mobile phones, and when the English Premier League has become the most popular weekly football attraction in the world.

There are those who argue that it is demeaning to think of people as brands: that to take something as complex, unpredictable and adaptable as a person and reduce them to the rudiments of a packaged product is distasteful and intellectually dishonest. I agree. People aren't brands, but – and it is a fine distinction – brands can be people. By that I mean that it is possible to manage the public side of your personality and, particularly in the case of celebrities, the commercialisation of your personal appeal in the same manner and with the same discipline as a successful brand.

Think about Beckham. How many of us know him? How many understand, or could even begin to imagine, what he thinks and feels at any moment in his life? But we all have a clear perception of him, and this perception is driven by what he does and the way he presents himself. And what he does is in turn driven by what he believes, what he values and what he wants to achieve in life.

This book is not a biography, nor even a psychological or sociological study of the Beckham phenomenon. Instead, it seeks to explain the success of Beckham as a brand by using the terms and analyses of modern brand management. I have tried to avoid academic or business jargon and to explain any marketing concepts in straightforward language to make this book as accessible as possible.

I hope *Brand it like Beckham* will appeal to those who know nothing about branding or marketing, but would like to understand these simple but incredibly influential concepts and the way companies use them. It should also appeal to people who know nothing about football but are interested in how the business of brands can be applied to social phenomena like soccer stars.

One final thought: I hope that when you finish reading this book, your respect and admiration for David Beckham and what he has achieved both as a footballer and as the first celebrity icon of the twenty-first century will be deepened. Beckham is a high-profile celebrity and as such lives under a 24-hour spotlight, with the media ready to jump on his every flaw and failing. For those of us who support the England team, let's hope he continues to lead it with the dedication and style and dignity he has brought to the game so far.

WARM UP

It is April 2004 and David Beckham is in the headlines for all the wrong reasons. A succession of women have revealed they have had affairs with the world's best-known soccer player and family man. Lurid details of the liaisons and text messages with graphic descriptions of intimate acts have dominated the tabloid press across the world. Beckham is reported to have confessed to Posh, and one newspaper alleges the couple are considering a split.

But it seems that the question on everyone's lips is not "Did he do it?" but "Will it damage his brand?" What a symptom of the marketing-dominated world we live in! We aren't concerned about how hurt his wife must be, or what the effect on his marriage is, or whether his kids are suffering; we're not even speculating about the likely impact on his on-pitch performance. No; in endless columns and hours of airtime, pundits like me are wheeled out to discuss the fall of Brand Beckham: the potential impact on his image, how sponsors may act, whether his brand can weather the storm.

We live in a world where we demand constant stimulation, seek instant gratification and pursue vicarious fulfilment through celebrity glamour – a world where brands provide us with a sense of identity, a shared language and a means of achieving our aspirations. Beckham's combination of glamour and marketing savvy has built a unique brand that is admired around the world by young and old, male and female. That's why we are so fascinated by this latest turn of events, and why we wonder whether that carefully constructed marketing creation that is the Beckham brand can survive . . .

1

BECKHAM THE PRODUCT STORY

Focus on what you are good at

It is August 1996 and I am watching **Match of The Day** in my front room, a half-drunk can of lager in my hand. I am beginning to doze off when suddenly something remarkable happens. A Man Utd player whose name I barely know receives the ball just inside his own half, and spotting the Wimbledon keeper far from his goal, unleashes a terrific shot that dips more than 60 yards into the goal. Astonishing! I leap out of my chair and stare at the screen. The player launches into a celebratory ritual that will become one of his trademarks: arms pulled back at right angles to the elbows, fists clenched, face fixed in a rictus of triumph. David Beckham has arrived unannounced in my consciousness, and he hasn't left it since.

David Beckham is a unique individual. A brilliant footballer, superb athlete, fashion icon, celebrity, model, soon-to-be-film star (it is rumoured). And he has now received the ultimate accolade of our consumer society: a "brand." He is so many different things. But what is he really about? What is the story of his success?

It is a fundamental truth that all great and enduring brands have at their heart a great product, one that is capable of developing over time. They must contain some genuine quality that people can recognise, respect and recommend. Once people experience a brand and like it, it acquires the legitimacy to offer them something else: maybe a different kind of product, but one with similarities in form or function or emotional resonance. Virgin has one great product in its record stores and another in its airlines, and these have allowed it to enter numerous other product areas where its values of having fun, being irreverent and championing the customer – values first established through the record shops – attract a loyal audience.

Despite all the hype that surrounds brands and branding, the law of customer demand still reigns supreme: if you don't have something worth buying, people won't buy it. So when we think about Beckham the brand, we must start by considering Beckham the product. What is it that he has done so well? What allows him to stay within the public consciousness? What gives him that fundamental legitimacy? Let's take a look at the life story of the brand named Beckham.

Getty Images

David Joseph Beckham was born on 2 May 1975 in Leytonstone, London. He showed talent as a footballer from an early age. He played for his local clubs and representative sides and soon attracted the attention of top scouts. He trialled with Leyton Orient (whose scores he still follows) and had talks with Tottenham, but was eventually signed as a trainee for Manchester United in 1991, at the age of 16. It was a dream come true; he had been a United fan as long as he could remember, and had met Bobby Charlton at a training session when he was just 11. His dad supported the team too, and would often buy his son shirts and merchandise bearing the Red Devils' logo.

From the beginning, Beckham showed remarkable determination in pursuing his dream of becoming a professional footballer. Early video footage shows the schoolboy Beckham selling his opponents short with a feint and dummy before sending a pass to his teammate – a move that would be repeated in years to come on grander stages than a London primary school's playing field.

Yet Beckham's career at Man Utd wasn't so spectacularly precocious as that of other team heroes; indeed, some pundits don't rate his playing highly at all. He wasn't a teenage wunderkind like George Best or Norman Whiteside or Ryan Giggs, all of whom burst onto the football scene at an age when most of their contemporaries were deciding whether to stay on at school for A levels. In fact, Beckham's league debut for Man Utd didn't come until he was 20, and he was 21 by the time he scored that goal against Wimbledon.

But he was dedicated and his sheer hard graft paid off before long. As Alex Ferguson, his manager at Man Utd, was to say later, "David Beckham is Britain's finest striker of the ball not because of God-given talent but because he practises with a relentless application ... practice might not make you perfect, but it will definitely make you better."[1] Dedication and commitment are themes we will return to in more depth when we look at the values of the Beckham brand.

Although he was a frequent starter for Man Utd during the 1995–96 season, it wasn't until the following season and that sensational goal against Wimbledon that he received worldwide attention. That season saw him establish himself as a permanent fixture in the Man Utd and England teams, and ended with his club winning the premiership for the fourth time. His status as a top footballer was cemented when he won the PFA Young Player of the Year award, and finished second in the Player of the Year poll. His meteoric rise in football stardom was accompanied by growing acclaim as a celebrity, thanks to his looks and his relationship with Victoria Adams of the Spice Girls (the "girl power" pop band then at the peak of its popularity). Intensifying media coverage, coupled with his rising popularity, made him an attractive proposition for marketers.

With his nonchalantly floppy hairstyle and determined style of play, Beckham had an appeal all his own: not a bad boy, more of a lovable rogue. Brylcreem signed him up to promote its haircare products to the teenage and young adult market in particular. Its association with a rising superstar gave its waning image a much-needed boost. So, if David was a late starter compared to other soccer heroes, he more than made up for it with the speed and trajectory of his take-off.

But the meteoric rise was almost followed by an equally spectacular crash. Beckham was sent off against Argentina in the second round of the 1998 FIFA World Cup. Vilified by the British public, he became the target of abuse in playing fields all over the country. He endured the criticism, earning respect for his attitude, and played a vital part in Man Utd's most successful season.

By the start of the 1999–2000 season, he had shaved off the famous blond locks for a shaven look. This made him irrelevant as a spokesperson for haircare products, and Brylcreem soon ended its association with him. While this season did not reap immediate commercial success, Beckham's successful recovery from the FIFA World Cup debacle, and especially his resilience in the face of criticism, went a long way in building up the core values of the Beckham brand. His excellent performances for Man Utd in another strong season consolidated his position as one of the best players in the country, as well as strengthening his appeal to marketers nationwide.

With the birth of his first son, Brooklyn Beckham, and his wedding to Victoria Adams in 1999, another key ingredient of the Beckham brand was put in place. Worldwide media coverage and public interest in his personal life ensured that Beckham's image as a doting father and loving husband won him many fans beyond football. Compared to other high-profile players of the time who had public battles with alcohol or drugs, Beckham had a relatively clean-living image, even when he was single. His dedication to his family was evident in the way he stood up to terrace crowds chanting abuse about his wife and child. His spats with Alex Ferguson over family commitments may not have done his Man Utd career any favours, but it earned him the sympathy and respect of the neutral fan, who tended to view Ferguson as the bully in these encounters.

His commercial success exploded at the turn of the decade after he had repeatedly proved himself a big-time player on the global football scene. With his appointment as captain of the England team in 2000, he became a role model for young footballers across the nation. His relationship with Victoria made him more comfortable in front of the camera and put him at ease with the idea of being a celebrity and not just a footballer. His widespread exposure in fashion magazines and the successful launch of his first book, *My World*, in 2000 gave worldwide audiences an insight into his eventful life. Marketers were quick to pick up on his popularity, and sponsorship deals were clinched one after another in the UK, Europe and the Far East, where football was becoming increasingly popular.

By 2003, there was endless speculation about the value that "brand Beckham" brought to companies, and indeed about how much it was worth in its own right. The figures are staggering. Beckham earned £15 million in advertising campaigns between May 2001 and May 2003. Sales of

Brylcreem shot up by 50 percent when he acted as its spokesman. In two separate surveys, the value of the Beckham brand was estimated at £60 million and £200 million. Whatever the actual value was, nobody could dispute that owning the Beckham trademark was a reliable way of making money.

The latest twist in his career came in summer 2003. Despite his obvious love for and loyalty to Manchester Utd and its fans (but no doubt goaded by his increasingly frosty relationship with Alex Ferguson), he left Old Trafford to join another legendary brand of football club: Real Madrid.

Beckham provided Real Madrid with a ready-made channel into Asia: a market where the popularity of football is enormous, as is the potential for merchandising, but where Real did not have a strong following. After it secured the Beckham brand, sales of Real Madrid merchandise – and especially the number 23 shirt – rocketed. Just as important, in case anyone thought the deal was strictly commercial, Beckham gave the team a width and an extra dimension to its midfield at a time when some observers thought Louis Figo's influence might be starting to wane, and the burden of performance might have fallen too heavily on Zinedane Zidane.

Predictably, the media tended to focus on the commercial and celebrity aspects of the move, and waited like hawks to pounce on any sign that Beckham the product (the footballer) would be exposed in a more competitive market (the Real Madrid first eleven, with its glittering array of talent).

Beckham had an indifferent start in his first two games, and the headlines predicting failure that had obviously been prepared the day he signed for Real were duly dusted down and brought out. But with his characteristic determination, Beckham set about concentrating on his football, settling in to the team and delivering goals and assists for goals that have already marked him out as one of Real's golden boys.

At the same time, Beckham made another decision that proves the rule that all brands must constantly focus on the quality and relevance of what they produce. Taking control of his life, he released a public statement that he was going to scale back his commercial activities so that he could focus entirely on football. He restructured his relationship with SFX, the marketing company that managed his commercial endorsements and brokered the Real Madrid deal, though he continued for the moment to work with SFX employee Tony Stephens, who had been his agent since Beckham was 20. (Stephens' company, whose clients included other soccer talent such as Alan Shearer and Michael Owen, had subsequently been bought by SFX.) This restructuring followed the decision to appoint pop impresario Simon Fuller, who had launched Victoria's career in the Spice Girls, to help build the husband-and-wife Beckham brand globally. At the same time, Beckham appointed Terry Byrne, director of football at Watford, as his personal manager. Finally he ended the relationship with Tony Stephens in January 2004.

This restructuring of Beckham's personal brand management is much like processes undergone by some corporate and product brands. At a certain stage, a brand can become so extended and its management so unfocused that a fundamental strategy review is undertaken to get back to core values or target new opportunities.

There has been a lot of speculation in the press and from interested parties about who is pulling the strings in this latest turn in the management of Beckham's affairs. Is it Posh? Is it Real Madrid? Did Adidas, one of Beckham's biggest sponsors, have a say? Is the new focus on football no more than spin?

The simple explanation is that David Beckham knows that his popularity and value are forged on the pitch; anything done to undermine his football will undermine everything else. So he has decided to leave others, including his wife, to manage his career as a celebrity. The fact that he is passionate about his sport and an exemplary dedicated professional seems to be lost on some of the press. Beckham loves playing football, and wants to be the best he can. That is the essence of the Beckham brand.

But it is also the source of the predicament that brand Beckham will face in years to come. What happens when he hangs up his boots, and the core product becomes irrelevant? Will management beckon? Will Hollywood call? Or will Beckham become famous for being famous, and exploit that fame for the general good or for personal gain?

At the end of each chapter, I will highlight the one key lesson we should take from it in terms of understanding both the Beckham brand and the principles of branding: a golden nugget, as it were, or better still, a "goldenball." So what basic principle do we learn from this chapter?

GOLDENBALL 1

To be a great brand, you have to have a great product in the first place: not necessarily a better product, but something that is different, that you are dedicated to and that you constantly strive to improve. Brands are like footballers in this respect: play off your past and you will soon be out of the team.

Notes
1   ESPN Soccernet website, 2001.

2

WHAT IS A BRAND, AND WHAT IS A CELEBRITY BRAND?

Learn from the experience of others

"Products rust, buildings age,
people die, but brands endure."

Attributed to Sir Hector Laing, former chairman of United Biscuits

"There are three laws of branding:
differentiate, differentiate, differentiate!"

Attributed to Roberto Goizueta, former CEO of Coca-Cola

We have set out on a journey to understand the Beckham brand, but before we go any further, we need to agree some terms of reference. What is a brand? How do companies build brands? Can celebrities use similar methods to build their own brands? What do we mean by a celebrity brand anyway?

Let's deal with the first question. What is a brand? The word "brand" has been so overused and misapplied that its meaning has become devalued. Most people think of a brand as first and foremost a logo or recognisable name. They associate brands with packaged goods, cars and other heavily advertised consumable or durable products. But brands are much more than that.

Think of Starbucks: it has a distinctive name and logo, but where is its advertising? Compared to other global brands such as Apple, BMW, Coke and Nokia, it hardly advertises at all. It doesn't need to; it has created such a strong customer experience on the high street that it breeds its own word-of-mouth recommendations. In fact, its stores are like living advertisements. Not only do they advertise the offer and promote the brand, they also invite you to come in and try the experience.

So a brand is not a logo or the product of a skilful advertising campaign. It is at once more simple and more complex than that. At its simplest, a brand is a symbol that guarantees a particular experience (a cup of coffee that you will enjoy; pleasant surroundings where you can relax). At its most complex, it is a blend of attributes that serve to distinguish one product, company, service, organisation or person from another. These attributes are both tangible (the taste and aroma of the coffee; the warmth of the café; the comfort of your chair) and intangible (a way of giving yourself a treat; a quiet moment in a busy day).

"Products are made in a factory; brands are made in the mind" is an article of faith among the marketing fraternity. It encapsulates the idea that although what you produce is vitally important (as we saw in the previous chapter), the product itself is not enough. How it is packaged and promoted, where and how it is sold, what price it sells for and, increasingly, how the people behave who represent that product (be it a sales assistant in a shop or a celebrity in an advert) all combine to create a profound impression in our mind that will help determine whether we prefer and remain loyal to a particular brand (see diagram). Once we understand a brand

Factors that influence perceptions of a brand

Source: Interbrand

in this way, we can see that anything that can be protected as a trademark can be a brand. Charities such as Oxfam and Greenpeace have just as much claim to be brands as IBM and BP and other companies do. Tiger Woods and David Beckham are no less branded products than a Coke or a Nokia phone.

Brands simplify complex experiences, allowing people to make rapid choices on a limited amount of information. In effect, they function as a kind of editor, shortening the process of selecting from a bewildering range of products and services, good causes and demands on our attention. This makes them very powerful. It also means that corporations must be constantly vigilant about the health of their brands. That's why so many corporations have adopted "Only do what is good for our brand" as their mantra. Their reasoning goes like this: if the people who are most important to us are the regular customers who keep buying our products or services, then focusing on what distinguishes our offerings in these people's minds – namely, the brand – is the best way for us to retain these customers and attract new ones in future.

The security of demand that brands bring to companies in this way is one of the main reasons why they are regarded as such valuable assets. Indeed, for many companies, their brand is their most valuable asset, one their entire business is designed to maintain and protect. The leading brand consultancy Interbrand conducts an annual survey of the world's most valuable brands (see table), and estimates that brands make up more than a third of the total value of all corporations.

Most valuable brands

Dollar value, 2003

1. Coca-Cola, $70.45 billion
2. Microsoft, $65.17 billion
3. IBM, $51.77 billion
4. GE, $42.34 billion
5. Intel, $31.11 billion
6. Nokia, $29.44 billion
7. Disney, $28.04 billion
8. McDonald's, $24.70 billion
9. Marlboro, $22.18 billion
10. Mercedes, $21.37 billion

Source: Interbrand

Celebrities, and in this case sports stars, clearly qualify as brands. Their names can be protected as trademarks; they have distinctive attributes that can be functional (bends a ball from 30 yards out like no one else) or emotional (charisma and charm); they have well-defined identities; and they command a loyal following that can endure long after their product has been superceded in the market.

We identify with and buy into celebrities for the same reasons we buy into brands. They add colour and excitement to our life. They provide a promise or a reassurance of a particular experience. We admire what they do, how they look or what they represent. They offer a shared frame of reference that enables us to bond with other people (get two strangers in a pub who discover they both like David Beckham and the conversation will flow as readily as the seven pints that will be consumed during it). Above all, celebrities provide a meaning or interest or sense of aspiration in our lives that few of us can supply on our own.

Indeed, the heroes we choose and our reasons for choosing them say more about us than about them. The humanistic psychologist Abraham Maslow spoke of people's need for "self-actualisation." I don't propose to go into Maslow's theories in detail, but his argument, put simply, is that those of us in highly developed economies where we no longer need to root around to satisfy our basic needs for food and shelter develop psychological needs for things like social acceptance and love. The ultimate need is self-actualisation: enhancing one's sense of self. This is why we don't market bottled water with the proposition that it quenches thirst (the most basic of Maslow's needs), but that it frees our spirit and gives us the lifestyle we aspire to attain. Daft when you think about it, but then we aren't logical creatures, are we?

BRAND PERSONALITY AND PERSONALITY BRANDS

Much of brand marketing is predicated on the need to create personality and values for inanimate objects (soap powders, fizzy drinks, cars) in order to encourage us to identify with the product and develop the same kind of loyalty that people show towards their heroes. Moreover, modern marketing communications often elect to dramatise the product or service to demonstrate how necessary it is to us. This dramatisation can range from the mundane (the child coming home from a party with a dirty shirt that only brand X detergent can get clean) to the exceptional (the child's life saved in a crash by the side-impact bars on brand Y car). In much the same way, sports star brands are created through moments of drama that are capable of keeping their emotional grip over us for years to come: even those of us who were barely crawling at the time still get misty-eyed at old TV footage of Geoff Hurst scoring England's fourth goal in the 1966 World Cup.

So for years brands aped personalities, whereas now personalities are becoming brands. The main difference is that branding is a business discipline that has been systematised for decades, whereas the process of marketing and branding personalities is relatively recent, and one of the more interesting developments in marketing. Even more interesting, though, is the extent to which these personalities have become their own brand managers. Let's take a look at the use of celebrities in marketing and branding, and the way it has developed.

Celebrity endorsements have been sought by manufacturers for their products since advertising began. The function of a celebrity endorsement is basically threefold:

1. It builds awareness. Linking a brand to a well-known name is an easy way of promoting it. This applies not just to the launch of new products, but also to the entry of established products into new markets. Often the

best way to get a new country to take up your brand is to find a local celebrity to endorse it.

2. It confers credibility. Ronald Reagan endorsed Chesterfield cigarettes in the 1950s, so they must have been good, mustn't they?

3. It adds or reinforces emotional and psychological attributes. Beckham is cool, so Brylcreem must be too.

For an endorsement to be successful, the celebrity has to be well known by the target market and relevant to the product. This is why the first products sport stars are asked to endorse are sports equipment: soccer boots, golf clubs, rugby balls. The target market will know the celebrity and be likely to believe the endorsement. For the same reason, film stars are often asked to endorse fashion or style items.

So far, so good. But then a celebrity's fame and image may suggest that there is a way of extending the product range that he or she is capable of endorsing. This is where the skill and judgement of agents and managers come into play. They are likely to pursue one of two strategies. "Earn till you burn" means that as a celebrity (and especially a sports star) you have a limited opportunity to make money, so get as much as you can as quickly as you can before you are finished. "Nurture the flame," on the other hand, means that if a celebrity's professional and public careers are properly managed and commercial choices are carefully considered, it is possible to prolong earning power and public prominence long after the celebrity's career has waned.

In the past, most celebrity (and particularly sports star) marketing took the "earn till you burn" approach. George Best's name appeared on everything from chewing gum to hair salons. No real thought was given as to what might be a suitable licensing or endorsement opportunity. Who cared? Everyone got paid.

Even now, you can still see a lot of this approach around the world. Why is Andre Agassi seen as a good choice for selling cars and phones? In Thailand, there isn't a brand from financial services to telecoms that doesn't use leading tennis player Paradorn Srichaphan to endorse its products or appear in its ads.

The problem with this approach is that celebrity fatigue soon sets in. A few individuals get so over-exposed that they no longer hold any charm for people. They also lose credibility. What does Agassi know about cars? What does he know about phones? Why should I, as a consumer, believe he is anything more than a marketing device designed to make me part with my cash as quickly as possible?

At the same time, sponsors, manufacturers and brand owners get concerned about the exclusive value that the celebrity is bringing to their brand. If the celebrity I am considering using is promoting anything and everything, how can I make my product stand out? How do I ensure that it is *my* product that benefits from the recognition and image transfer, and not everyone else's? As we will see in the next chapter, there is already a danger that Beckham has been too exposed too soon, which could damage his earning potential and value to sponsors. Perhaps he had good reason to announce his intention to focus on football matters.

American businesses spent $897 million on sports star endorsements in 2001 alone. That's a lot of money going to a small number of people. Because these sums are so vast, companies need systematically to evaluate their return on investment. How exactly am I, as a sponsor, benefiting from associating with this sports star? Might I be able to enjoy the same benefit from another celebrity or from some other form of merchandising or marketing activity?

Many companies have now made sponsorships and celebrity endorsements part of their overall strategy rather than a tactical marketing activity. They have become much more particular in deciding which celebrity to use where, how often and for how long. Indeed, many have brand blueprints that they use to identify the right kind of celebrity and the best treatment of that celebrity for their brand. Such a blueprint would probably cover the following points:

- Fit between the celebrity's and the brand's values
- Fit between the celebrity's and the brand's personality
- Fit between the celebrity's public and private life and the target customer's perceptions
- Tone of voice and vocabulary to be used in relation to the celebrity
- Types of activity that are appropriate or inappropriate for the celebrity
- Reasons for removing celebrity as brand spokesperson.

By asking a series of questions about each celebrity in this way, companies hope to guard against costly mistakes. After all, the problem with using a celebrity to speak for you is that you have no control over what they get up to. That is why morals clauses are routinely included in contracts between companies and the celebrities they use.

If companies are becoming more strategic about their approach to sponsorship, so too are the celebrities themselves. In the past, a celebrity's main responsibility in endorsing products was to turn up at the advertising shoot, read the cue card, attend the PR event, stay sober and then take the money (minus agent's commission). Today, many celebrities realise that they can create their own brand and therefore need to manage it carefully.

Think of Paul Newman: he stopped endorsing the products of others a long time ago, preferring to exploit his name and the brand values associated with it for himself, through such products as his salad sauces. Liz Taylor has her name on perfumes. Greg Norman and his great white shark logo adorn bottles of his own fine wines. Tiger Woods should be exploring his own brand of golf goods. It is a logical step: Tiger Woods made Nike millions by lending his image to its products, so why not cut out the middle man and launch his own range?

Managing oneself as a celebrity brand is a more complex undertaking than managing a product personality is for a company. For a start, a celebrity brand is prominently on view and exposed to public opinion for much of the time.

Although celebrities achieve their right to be in people's minds by their core skill or activity, as we discussed in chapter 1, they maintain their position and extend or deepen the public's affection by everything they do, personal as well as professional, private as well as public. The world probably doesn't much care whether the CEO of some major multinational has an affair or not; even if he were convicted of a crime, it is unlikely it would register on consumers' radar screens. But if David Beckham is seen at the same nightclub as an attractive girl when Posh isn't there, then the whole carefully constructed edifice that is brand Beckham comes under public attack.

So managing a celebrity brand is not just about choosing which products to endorse or causes to support. It is also about how to act as a parent, spouse, friend, child. This doesn't mean that all celebrity brands have to be squeaky clean like Beckham; Vinnie Jones can rampage on a plane and still be regarded as "on brand." It does mean, though, that a celebrity who is serious about being a brand has to think carefully about every choice he or she makes in private life as well as public appearances.

THE GEORGE FOREMAN STORY

A recent example of a star who has become a household brand for reasons other than the sport that made him famous is George Foreman. A charismatic character as well as a successful boxer, Foreman made what proved to be his most lucrative career move when he signed a deal in the mid-1990s with an obscure appliance manufacturer called Salton. Eight years later, he had turned a strange-looking grill into one of the best-selling household appliances of all time. More than 40 million George Foreman Lean, Mean, Fat-Reducing Grilling Machines have been sold in less than a decade, with sales rocketing from $5 million in 1996 to $400 million in 2002.

People have speculated about the reasons for this success, but they all come back to three key factors: awareness, credibility and image. George Foreman supplied awareness because everyone knew his name. He supplied credibility because as a heavyweight boxer he had to eat hearty food such as steaks, and people could see that he ate what he sold. In one memorable moment on QVC, he started tucking into the food from the grill, unaware that the TV cameras were on him. Finally, Foreman supplied a charisma that a steel grill patently lacks.

It's interesting to consider why Foreman should have chosen this product opportunity and not others. First, he could use his own name to make money; second, but just as important, he could sell something he believed in. The original deal with Salton gave him a 45 percent share of the profits and no upfront payment, so he had to believe in the product, as he would only get paid if it sold well for some time. When the terms of the contract were later renegotiated because Foreman's profit share was preventing the company from investing and expanding, he agreed to sell Salton the rights to use his name for US$17.5 million, but he also insisted on continuing to act as the salesman for the product, even though he was not contractually obliged to. He felt the product was right for him and his image, and having given his name to it, he could not walk away. That sincere and fervent commitment is the hallmark of great brand managers everywhere.

THE SIX ELEMENTS OF BRAND BUILDING

So celebrities are now becoming proper managers of their own brands. What then are the issues they have to think about? What are the key disciplines of brand management: the tools and techniques, thought processes and best practices that have created strong brands? Essentially, brand building can be whittled down to the following elements:

1. Definition of what the brand stands for

Brands have values (positive attributes that are distinctive and relevant to people), personality (characteristic ways of communicating) and purpose (customer-focused goals or objectives). Defining them clearly is the single most important task for a brand manager: unless you know what you are and what you want to be, you will have no idea what you should be doing and how you should do it. As marketing folk like to put it, you will not know how you want to be positioned in people's minds.

2. Creation of the brand's visual and verbal style (logo, imagery, language)

Every great brand has a memorable brand name, logo, colour, set of graphic imagery and tone of voice in written and spoken communications that sets it apart from everyone else. Think of the distinctive aesthetics of a Gap advert, a BMW dealership or a Disney store. Attention to detail and consistency of delivery in the presentation of brand identity and communications are the signs of a great brand.

3. Delivery of the brand through the product or service and customer experience as a whole

The products or services that a brand selects and offers, their quality, where they are sold and how they are sold are all proof of the brand's promise. In your relationship with customers, the moment of truth is not when someone sees your advert but when they experience your offering. But having a good product (a car that doesn't break down, gets you from A to B, goes from 0 to 60 in six seconds) is not enough. It is the way that the product is presented that often makes the biggest difference to the customer.

4. Management of the brand's return on investment

If you don't measure it, how do you know if it's working? There are numerous ways of assessing whether a brand is having the desired effect on its customers; the most important is understanding the contribution it makes to company profitability.

5. Identification of new opportunities, ventures and initiatives for the brand

Brands are not single products; they are mental constructs and can assume different forms over time. Kodak sells photocopiers now, but started out selling Box Brownie cameras. A brand owner's understanding of its brand will affect the choices it makes in new product development and in joint ventures and co-branding with other companies.

6. Protection of intellectual property

A brand is a specific piece of legal title. If you don't protect it properly at law and ensure that no one can infringe it, then you are investing in something that your competitors can benefit from.

These, then, are the key elements that we will use to frame our assessment of David Beckham the brand in the rest of this book.

GOLDENBALL 2

Managing a brand is a systematic process covering a multiplicity of factors. Celebrities are no longer just endorsers of other people's products; they are brands in their own right, and are learning how to manage themselves as such.

3

DEFINING THE BECKHAM BRAND

Be clear about what you stand for

"A brand is what people say about you when you are not in the room"

Jeff Bezos, Amazon CEO

The world loves Beckham not merely for what he does, but for who he is. When he wears a sarong, it says something about his style; when he meets Nelson Mandela, it says something about his values; when he scores those goals against Greece or Argentina, it speaks volumes of his dedication, his passion and his commitment. But can we understand exactly what it is that people like about him?

What does our brand mean to people, and what do we want it to mean? What does it stand for? What is it that people value about it, and what do they dislike? These are the kinds of question that marketers wrestle with long into the night. To some people, they might seem trivial, pretentious or downright daft. What personality can a chocolate bar have? What meaning can there be in a box of soap powder, other than to wash clothes? But brand building goes way beyond product performance, and the associations people have with brands are often engendered by factors other than the product itself.

The key dimensions of Beckham's life that affect our perceptions of him

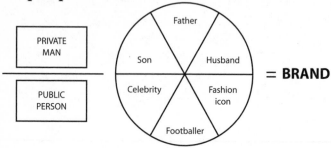

Marketers try to define the brand they want very closely, and use a combination of research and intuitive judgements to reach their definition. Through this process, brands become personified, with goals, values and personalities that help to shape and control their behaviour. There are a number of conceptual tools and intellectual models that companies use to help with this definition. Basically, they are all concerned with answering the same question: what do we want our brand to stand for?

Great brands have a very clear and aspirational reason for being that transcends pure product function. Apple is not about making computers, but about liberating human creativity. Disney is not about making cartoons, but about creating magic for kids of all ages. For a brand to achieve its purpose, it has to act in certain ways, and the ways it acts are informed by its values. So for Apple, creativity is a positive thing that shapes the way it designs products and communicates with others. For Disney, the theme of "no cynicism" shapes the way it writes screenplays and runs its theme parks.

Then there is the personality that influences the way a brand speaks and looks. The Apple brand is young and challenging; the Disney brand is an ageless child. Next comes a brand's "area of competence," or what it can legitimately endorse. For Apple, all forms of computing-related technology that empower human creativity can be branded with its logo. For Disney, anything that is wholesome family fun can bear the Disney name. (When Disney makes films with adult themes, it uses a separate brand, Touchstone Pictures, to ensure that its brand promise to consumers is never confused.)

Finally, there is the positioning or "space in the mind" that the brand wants to capture. This is not the same as market position, which is an objective and quantifiable result of business activities ("We are number 1 in the market for personal computers"). Rather, it is about people's perceptions or mental images of a brand's key differentiating benefit (such as "the best computers for creative people").

So where does that leave David Beckham? What does his brand stand for? Has he set out with single-minded determination to build a lasting brand, and has he succeeded?

To help find out, we conducted some research with football fans around the world. We were interested in understanding what Beckham meant to them. But we also looked at what Beckham has said and done: how he has shaped, deliberately or otherwise, these perceptions. The results can be seen in the table at the end of this chapter.

We discovered that there are three main attributes that cut across all areas of Beckham's life and strengthen his appeal: dedication, an iconic sense of style and a down-to-earth humanity.

DEDICATION

This is the first and most important of Beckham's key attributes. People used many different words to describe it:

commitment, determination, loyalty; hard-working, professional, relentless. And they used phrases to match: "He gives 110 percent"; "He is always the most committed man on the field"; "Look how much he gives for England"; "He put his kid and his wife first."

Beckham may not have the natural flair and charisma of Eric Cantona or George Best, or the electrifying skill and pace of Ryan Giggs; rather, his dedication has been his biggest asset. He has worked and worked at his game to ensure he is never carried by his team, but if anything carries it. In this respect, the footballer he most resembles is Kevin Keegan, a player not blessed with the prodigious talent of such contemporaries as Rodney Marsh, Tony Currie and Frank Worthington, but who achieved far more than they did thanks to his relentless pursuit of greatness.

The people who took part in our research revealed a qualified appreciation of Beckham's talent. Some regarded him as the best midfielder in the world. Others thought him overrated. But whether they were fans or sceptics, everyone agreed that it was his hard work that made the difference. "He's not the greatest footballer in terms of skill, but he is the best at dedicating himself." "Zidane and Figo are better pure-quality players, but with Beckham you know he will always give 100 percent." As Jorge Valdano, Real Madrid's sporting director, said, "Beckham is a great professional. He loves football and he dedicates himself to his profession exclusively."[1]

1 Notes appear at the end of each chapter.

We can test such verdicts against our own experiences. Remember Beckham in that 2001 FIFA World Cup qualifying game for England against Greece. He ran around the pitch, dragging his team mates into the game, cajoling, coaxing and eventually kicking them to qualification. It was a natural, uncontrived display of his character and personality: the values he holds dear dramatised at a moment when there was no place to hide. This is what people remember about Beckham, and why so many people like him.

His dedication makes Beckham an ideal spokesman for many sports brands. In late 2003, Adidas adverts in Europe and Asia showed Beckham and Johnny Wilkinson (the Beckham of rugby) practising their kicks. By showing these stars dedicating themselves to their craft, Adidas was tapping into people's respect and admiration for authentic sports performers.

It was his dedication to being a great footballer that saw Beckham through the most difficult phase in his career: the fall-out after he was sent off in the Argentina match during the 1998 FIFA World Cup. It is hard to remember now, but the contempt and scorn poured out on this floppy-haired 23-year-old were almost unprecedented; other soccer personalities didn't receive such abuse until they got to be grey-haired managers. Papers that are now proud to bear his image were inviting readers to use his photo as a dartboard. Beckham admits it was a dark time, but he bore the enormous pressure without cracking. He came back for the 1998–99 season and dedicated himself to improving his game and helping club and country qualify for the European finals.

His dedication to Manchester United and its fans is one of the reasons why his transfer took so long. Had his relationship with Alex Ferguson not deteriorated, and had the team not needed to raise cash to fill gaps in other parts of the pitch, Beckham might still be playing for Man Utd today. Who is to say that he won't return to Old Trafford? Other United legends have, from Denis Law to Mark Hughes.

But it's not just in his football that Beckham shows his dedication. His marriage may be one of the most high-profile relationships in the world, but close friends regard it as a genuine match, and not just a marriage arranged by marketing. That doesn't mean it won't suffer the highs and lows any relationship goes through, especially if it is conducted in the glare of the media spotlight where there is little room to hide. But certainly after they first met and for their first few years together, Beckham made a virtue of his public devotion to Posh and the kids. When he had the first of his very public falling-outs with Ferguson, it was over his decision to spend time with his son Brooklyn in order to support his wife while she was in London. When we conducted focus group research in Asia in 2003, people still remembered that moment, and there was no doubt where their sympathies lay: "Beckham was looking out for his wife; that shows he is about more than just the money"; "If football was everything to him, he wouldn't have done that."

It is as a father that the dedication people associate with Beckham gets its most emotional acclaim. His devotion to his children is universally recognised and admired. People may laugh at the funny names he has given his kids – although personally I think Brooklyn is rather a nice name for a boy – but they respect his pride in his children and his readiness to show it in public.

Why is this dedication of Beckham's so important in terms of his brand image? It's simple: consumers (people like you and me) have become more marketing-literate, and consequently more sceptical of the claims that companies make for their products and services. We are hostile to anything that smacks of spin. We are fed up with hype. We hate to feel we have been taken in. We want the evidence of our own experience and the reassurance of our friends or peer group.

It isn't that we dislike marketing as such. In fact, most of us enjoy the paraphernalia of marketing: we like great packaging and branding, we enjoy clever ads and we love walking into stores with that special ambience. But none of it counts for anything unless there is a degree of authenticity or distinctiveness to support it all. Put simply, we like great products with great marketing, and not the latter without the former.

Beckham's dedication to his craft and his family strikes a chord with many people. It shows in everything he does and gives him the legitimacy to build his brand.

ICONIC SENSE OF STYLE

While dedication is the basis of Beckham's ability to appeal to a wide group of people, it is his iconic sense of style that divides Beckham likers from Beckham lovers, and can also turn people right off. We will look at how it is expressed in his physical appearance in the next chapter; here I want to concentrate on what it means at a psychological or behavioural level. Why is it so important to him and his brand? I use the word iconic advisedly; it means having the quality of an icon. Everything that Beckham wears or does has that quality, from his free kick, which has now been captured in the form of a logo, to his hairstyles, which define the various phases of his career. He is deliberate and often provocative in his choice of dress and in the way he plays football. This creates a unique set of symbols around him.

Look at the way he plays football. Beckham has always shown a preference for the flamboyant as long as it has a practical purpose. Man Utd would have appealed to him because it is the only team in England that has consistently maintained an ethos of playing entertaining football since the days of Sir Matt Busby. According to Paddy Crerand, a renowned player of the 1960s:

"We might win 1–0 and it wouldn't be attractive. [Sir Matt] would get very angry about it. 'The public have not come to watch this! They want to be entertained – that's what it is all about. If you enjoy it, then the crowd out there watching must enjoy it as well.'" [2]

You can say many things about Man Utd, but never that they are boring to watch.

As a footballer, Beckham specialises in a particular skill that is sublime to watch: the free kick that bends around a defensive wall and past the flailing arms of a beaten keeper. It's one of the most beautiful and dramatic shots in any sport, combining accuracy and speed in a trajectory that is virtually symmetrical from the point it leaves the ground to the moment the net stops its movement. But it isn't just the free kicks; his pin-point crosses and long diagonal cross-field passes are not only brilliant pieces of play, but aesthetically pleasing, a display of supreme craft. And he never looks less than wonderfully turned out on the pitch.

The sense of style inherent in Beckham's game is equally evident, but more controversial, off the field. The haircuts, the sarong, the increasingly upscale wardrobe and even his choice of spouse speak of a personality that has always appreciated stylishness. "Clothes are just one way of expressing your individuality, but it's an important one for me. I also think of dressing as a way of being artistic, and art is something that I'm quite into."[3]

Though it endeared him to the fashionistas, his interest in clothes played a part in turning many ordinary football supporters against him. Some saw him as a poseur, somebody who would rather flounce around in a skirt than put in the graft on the pitch. It is a tribute to Beckham that he has largely succeeded in overcoming this prejudice without ever abandoning his belief in the importance of style, whether expressed through his dress sense, grooming or style of play. People now accept that his fashion sense is a genuine part of who he is, and because he has proved his worth on the pitch, few accuse him of being all image and no skill.

Just as Beckham's dedication chimes with a modern sensibility that wants authenticity in its heroes, so his sense of style suits a time when men enjoy dressing up. The rise of the "metrosexual" – an urban heterosexual man characterised by sensitivity and a keen dress sense – is not entirely due to Beckham, but he has been at the vanguard of this trend. Men have become increasingly conscious of fashion, style and personal appearance. Marketers have been promoting grooming products for men since the mid-1990s, when the phenomenon of the SNAG (sensitive new-age guy – remember him?) first emerged. Shops offering an assortment of male fashions have burgeoned, each targeted at different lifestyles, attitudes and design preferences, from Gap to Diesel, Blazer to French Connection. Even soccer hooligans now wear Burberry. It's a mark of a society where people have less and less time and more and more money that cash gets lavished on luxury items, fashion statements, and things that make you look and feel good during the precious few hours when you are not working.

Some maintain that Beckham is a fashion leader and that he is heavily involved in the industry, helping to shape attitudes and design styles. Admittedly, he does set trends (from sarongs to Mohicans), but only after they have been invented or adopted by others. He has been described as a billion-dollar mannequin. Designers remark that what the fashion industry sees on the catwalk is faithfully replicated six months later by Beckham.

He also feeds off cultural influences such as hip hop, as can be seen in his choice of a Bentley, diamond studs and tattoos. Because he is a mainstream figure, people assume he is leading the way; in reality, though, he is an interface between high fashion, the true trendsetters (such as rappers) and the mass market. Beckham is ideal for this role – as many marketers have obviously spotted – not only because he looks good but because he is humane, tolerant of other lifestyles and unafraid of sensitivity. "I think it is good for men to be in touch with their feminine side," he told reporters in South Africa in 2003.

Moreover, his boyish blond looks, his flair for style and rumoured penchant for wearing his wife's underwear have made him something of a gay icon. When asked about it in a South African newspaper, Beckham earned himself more popularity among gays by saying he was "perfectly comfortable" with this status. Indeed, his wife was reported on the abcnews website as saying, "He's a big flirt and he loves it. He walks around the kitchen going: 'I'm a gay icon. I'm a gay icon.'"

Beckham seems unique in his ability to appeal to almost everyone: men love him, women love him, old folks adore him, young kids idolise him, straight guys copy him and gay guys treat him as an icon. Like the late Diana, Princess of Wales, he has been able to reach out and touch the widest possible range of communities. Everyone can see something in him to admire. And the reason he can hold all these disparate people together is because he strikes them as genuine, just as Diana always seemed to have the common touch. Which brings us to his third brand value. . .

DOWN-TO-EARTH HUMANITY

It may seem odd to use this phrase of a man who commands megabucks, has a pop-star wife who calls him Goldenballs, regularly adorns the cover of celebrity magazines and was splashed all over the tabloids for allegedly having sex with at least two girls while married, but it is true. Beckham does not engage in wild drinking binges like George Best, or leap into crowds and spout existentialist poetry like Cantona, or sexually abuse women like some English footballers. Even the women who alleged he slept with them paid tribute to his gentleness and decency as a lover and his ordinariness as a man. His lifestyle is undoubtedly lavish, but his approach to life is essentially modest. Beckham has for a long time been Mr Clean; he may not be the most charismatic of personalities, but while he has enough street cred to remain relevant to young people, his generally personable image ensures he is unlikely to bring any brand associated with him into disrepute.

Despite his celebrity lifestyle, Beckham remains level-headed about his fame, and has always put it into the broader context of his life: "My football is really important to me, but my son and my wife are the most important things to me in the world. And that's what fatherhood does to you. You don't realise how much you can love someone until then. It's a totally different kind of love."[4] As a spokesman for Man Utd and England, he has always come across as sensible, and his many TV appearances reveal him as self-deprecating and softly spoken. Although he is no wit or raconteur, he possesses an easy manner and pleasant personality. He has obviously taken sound advice to be himself and let his natural niceness shine through. Someone once observed drily that "Beckham is a brand until he speaks," but our research found that his lack of fluency made people warm to him, and his mild inarticulacy served to make him more genuine in their eyes.

Moreover, his emotional honesty has won him friends the world over. He may not have blubbed like Gazza, but when he does cry, it looks like the real thing. Gazza's emotional outpourings became embarrassing over the years, but Beckham's moods never are. When his children were born, he looked truly happy; during the Ferguson boot row, he seemed genuinely troubled. Reuters quoted public relations expert Karen Osbourne as saying: "People have a compassion for him because he has not always been a hero through and through. When he cried, when he had problems, when he was sent off, people certainly felt compassion for him."

Beckham's emotional honesty is very much in tune with our time. It seems that a fortunate combination of circumstances has made him the ideal candidate for first icon of the twenty-first century. Endless self-help books, Hollywood films, TV soaps and magazines have encouraged men to show how they really feel. They have learnt that far from making them look weak, this makes them more appealing.

Beckham's values directly shape his personality and people's perceptions of it. Our research shows that David

Beckham's brand personality is that of a man who is passionate about the things he believes in and dedicated to his art. He is stylish and individualistic, refusing to conform to conventional social norms for masculinity. Being a charismatic leader, he is comfortable in the spotlight and a natural role model for his peers.

But what about the Beckham brand's purpose in life? This is straightforward, and shines out in his autobiography and in everything he does. Beckham's *raison d'être* is the constant pursuit of excellence on and off the field; his mission is to be the greatest footballer he can: "All the other lads just wanted to go out drinking cider and doing whatever. I was at home watching *Match of the Day* on Saturday nights ... I've always been focused on my football. I knew what I wanted and I knew what I had to do to achieve it." [5] Excellence is what drives him and prompts his actions.

To see how different Beckham is, compare him with two other bearers of the iconic number 7 shirt for Manchester United. You could argue that George Best and Eric Cantona were more talented than Beckham; indeed, Best is perhaps the greatest instinctive footballer who ever played the game in Britain. But think of them as brands: what did they stand for? What did they do? How did they benefit themselves and others?

Cantona was all Gallic arrogance and flair, married to a fiery temper and a poet's soul. He lacked the dedication to make it at the highest international level, and the common touch to make him popular as a spokesman or endorser. And in any case, he wasn't interested; the commercialism of the game never suited him as it does Beckham.

But the more telling comparison is with Best, because it shows us how far the management of sports stars has come. Best had everything Beckham had, perhaps more: he was precocious, gifted and a visionary on the pitch. And like Beckham, he was blessed with great looks and a good head of hair. Best was the fifth Beatle, just as Becks seemed like a sixth Spice Girl in his sarong.

But as brands, they had different values and personalities, and were managed in different ways. Best displayed dilettantism, Beckham shows dedication; Best had a sense of show, Beckham a sense of style; Best liked the low life, Beckham has a common touch; Best has an addictive personality, Beckham a driven one. Both are cheeky and passionate about their sport, but whereas Beckham is comfortable with his celebrity status, Best seems to have been destroyed by his fame.

The way they were commercially managed reflected these brand personalities. Best's name was everywhere and on everything. He even had his own clothes shop. Nobody though, was managing his image or thinking about his future in any systematic way. In fact, nobody thought about him as a brand. If they had, they might have given him better advice about what to endorse, what categories to go into, where to develop, how to protect his image, why he should focus on his game, how to prolong his career and even what he should do afterwards. After all, brand building is a long-term endeavour. Beckham benefits from professional advice that

probably wasn't available to Best – but then again, they are such different characters that perhaps Best wouldn't have been able to take such advice.

Beckham as a brand is a perfect symbol for our times. His brand values of dedication, style and down-to-earth honesty accord perfectly with people's desire for authenticity, spectacle and a figure they can relate to and understand. His hunger to be the best and his balancing of professional and personal commitments appeal to our aspirations and allow us to identify with a common human predicament. His looks have given him a passport into the pages of the press, but it is his values that have won him a place in people's hearts.

In sum, the positioning that Beckham has achieved in people's minds could best be described as "the most stylish and dedicated celebrity sports icon of his time, who has bridged the worlds of fashion and football."

Notes

1 ESPN Soccernet website, June 2003.
2 *Uncommon Practice*, edited by Andy Milligan and Shaun Smith, FT Prentice Hall, 2002.
3 *Sunday Times*, South Africa, June 2002.
4 *Sunday Times*, South Africa, 5 May 2002.
5 *Sunday Times*, South Africa, 5 May 2002.

GOLDENBALL 3

Brands are built on core values that people admire, and are communicated through a personality that people like. Celebrity brands are just the same; they have to be clear about their purpose and values, and act accordingly.

MULTIPLE DIMENSIONS OF THE BECKHAM BRAND

Through a combination of focus groups and questionnaires completed over the internet from October to December 2003, we sought to obtain a picture of what people think about David Beckham in his many roles. This table includes comments from football fans and consumers in general that capture the most commonly held views.

What are the words you immediately associate with Beckham?

Looks
Unisex appeal
Trendy
"Metrosexual"
Stylish
Mix of style and sport
Vain
Hair authority
Trendsetter
Honorary black man with soul
Iconic
Cult leader
Handsome
Earring
Beautiful person

Football
Free kick
One-dimensional
Right-legged
Real Madrid
Manchester United
Diver

Character
Dedicated
Quiet
Hard-working
Seeks attention but not naturally comfortable under it
Leader
"Wussy" voice
Meek
Squeaky voice
Captain

Family
Henpecked husband
Victoria

Marketing
Media tool
The Michael Jordan of football
Adidas

Let's consider Beckham's various roles. What do you think about:

David Beckham the footballer?
Class in his own right. Good peripheral vision and gifted crossing skills
Arguably the most effective dead-ball specialist in the game
Love his free kicks because of the unpredictability of the outcomes
Skilful and inspirational
Great crossing ability
Strong fighting spirit
Rises to the occasion
Hard-working, with strong leadership qualities

What are his key values as a footballer?
Performance/achievement
Dedication/commitment
Focus
Skill/talent

David Beckham the England captain?
Quiet leader
Takes young players under his wing
Big-game temperament
Matured into the role

What are his key values as a captain?
Patriotism
Patience
Nurturing care
Maturity
Ambition

David Beckham the father?
Doting
Loving
Protective
His tattoos (Guardian angel across his shoulders overlooking the name
Brooklyn at his hips) symbolise his love for his children

What are his key values as a father?
Kinship
Devotion
Passion

David Beckham the husband?
Tolerant
Loving
Faithful
Sweet

What are his key values as a husband?
Passion
Modern-day man
Sexual equality
Fidelity
Understanding

David Beckham the son?
Strong ties with his parents
Filial
Living out his dad's dream on the pitch

What are his key values as a son?
Filial piety
Respect
Family-oriented

David Beckham the celebrity and fashion icon?

Looks enigmatic and regal, yet projects a down-to-earth working-class image

Squeaky voice may be a turn-off, but it shatters his aura of invulnerability and makes him appeal to ordinary people

A product succeeding through superb packaging; good looks account for the bulk of his success

His marriage is a union of two celebrities that provides constant fodder for media coverage and boosts his exposure

He was in the right place at the right time

Victoria was behind his transformation from a shy man to a metrosexual icon

Undeniable star quality

Self-made millionaire; a good success story.

Versatile and able to look good in most situations

What are his key values as a celebrity and fashion icon?

Individuality

Confidence

Versatility

Hard work

Luck

David Beckham the marketing medium?

Pepsi ad (Beckham gives up shirt to boy who asks for it) portrays him as being very accommodating to his fans

Attention-grabbing

Adidas ad (free kick into a hole in an artificial wall) portrays him as a master of his art Marketing machine

People like the ads because he's in them, but they don't necessarily want to buy the goods

What are his key values as a marketing medium?

Creativity

Flair

Expertise

Charisma

Achievement

Victory

David Beckham the role model?

Not a natural role model in his younger days but grew into the role

First amongst equals (fellow British sportsmen); recognised beyond the football fraternity

Definitely a role model, and getting better at it. Temper under control and maturity growing

What are his key values as a role model?

Leadership

Compassion

Charisma

Exemplary behaviour

Maturity

Strength of character

4

BECKHAM'S BRAND IDENTITY

Make your looks count

"Don't f*** with the logo."

Attributed to head of major international petroleum company during a brand review

"This Gaultier-saronged, Posh spiced, Cool Britannia, look-at-me, what-a-lad, loadsamoney, sex-and-shopping, fame-schooled, daytime-TV, over-coiffed twerp."

Daily Telegraph, 2 July 1998

Like no other soccer star or maybe even sports star before him, Beckham has become a branded icon. He has great looks, he wears great clothes and as for his hair, well… He is the first footballer to have straddled the worlds of football and fashion and not looked awkward in either. When you talk about Beckham, many images spring to mind; as we see in this chapter, that's no accident. There is a design behind his design, as it were. He manages his image with a care that most modern branded goods firms would admire.

Brand identity – the symbols, signs, language, images and colours that a brand uses to distinguish itself in a market – is what most people think of when they hear the word "brand." It is the most important part of the marketing mix used to communicate a brand. If your brand name, logo and imagery are not differentiated, memorable and appealing, customers will not be able to find, buy and recommend you.

A brand's identity becomes a symbol that captures every positive experience or association that people have with the product or service or company it represents. This is what marketers call the "equity" in your brand, or what people find valuable about you that makes them carry on buying you. Because it is so important, companies employ people whose sole job it is to ensure that the brand identity is appropriately and consistently used whenever and wherever it appears. Often jokingly referred to as "logo cops," these people have a thankless task, but one that is vital to ensuring that customers can easily find the brand they are looking for, and that no other company can copy it.

The big challenge brand owners face in maintaining their brand identity is how to retain its consistency and (especially if it has been around for many years) its heritage, while keeping it fresh and contemporary, and ensuring the imagery stays relevant to changing tastes. If you are Shell or BMW or McDonald's, for example, you have a logo and colour scheme that people have known for decades. So how do you honour this heritage without allowing the brand to appear outdated?

Disney is one brand that has been able constantly to refresh its identity without compromising its heritage. Its success rests on two main achievements. First, it has been able to update the distinctive Walt Disney signature: while still closely resembling the original, the new version has a 3D feel that makes it seem more modern. Second, the company has cleverly organised the iconography associated with Disney into an identity system that is fresh, flexible and conveys personality: consider Mickey Mouse's head and ears silhouette, the sorcerer's apprentice, the fairytale castle.

Just as some brand symbols and logos endure, the themes of some advertising campaigns linger in the memory long after the ads themselves have been dropped. These themes worked for a short time because they captured the mood of the moment and were relevant to the brand, but they eventually become outdated, to be replaced by some other image or trendy reference. Cast your mind back to those wonderful Levi's adverts in the 1980s featuring the gorgeous hunk washing his jeans in the launderette; think of "Beanz meanz Heinz"; remember Audi's "Vorsprung durch Technik" campaigns. The skill is to express your brand personality in a relevant and fashionable way while letting your essential brand values and identity evolve slowly.

So it is with Beckham. His brand identity is one of his most celebrated and even parodied aspects, but it shows all the hallmarks of a cleverly conceived and well-managed brand strategy.

Let's start with the building block of his brand identity: his name (or rather names):

- David Beckham
- Beckham
- Becks
- DB.

Often the hardest job for any marketer faced with a new product is to work out what to call it. It sounds so simple, but it can tie whole companies up in knots as they try to find a name that captures all the glorious things they stand for. They may well find they need at least 12 words to do the job, like the characters in *Nicholas Nickleby* who decide to call their company the United Metropolitan Improved Hot Muffin and Crumpet Baking and Punctual Delivery Company, reasoning that "the very name will get the shares up to a premium in ten days." Faced with this problem, marketers often resort to a name that has the benefit of being short, unusual and memorable, but doesn't actually mean anything, like Kodak or Xerox.

If you had to come up with a great name for a football star, would you choose "David Beckham"? Think of the magical names of heroes like Pele and Maradona, the alliterative Kevin Keegan, the symbolic George Best, even the lyrical Eric Cantona (ooh ah Cantona). Other sports have players with evocative names like "Magic" Johnson and Tiger Woods, or exciting nicknames like The Fridge. But "David Beckham" sounds what it is: a dull Essex-boy name. And his nickname, Becks, is like a parody of the tradition of abbreviating footballers' names in the most pedestrian way possible: Shilton becoming Shilts, Robson Robbo, Hoddle Hod, and so on.

But if we think back to the previous chapter and Beckham's brand values – especially his down-to-earth ordinary appeal and authenticity – we can see that this very ordinariness suits the brand extremely well. Best was as charismatic and unique as his name suggests; Kevin Keegan as dynamic as the alliteration hints; Cantona a maestro. In the marketing of the Beckham brand, there has been no attempt to apologise for the remarkable ordinariness of the man; on the contrary, it has been a positive asset. He is just a normal bloke who shows what you can achieve with talent, dedication and good looks. His brand names are thus a perfect fit with his brand image.

"Beckham is such a down-to-earth guy; I can think of few sportsmen who appeal to as many different people as he does," was a comment from one of the members of our focus groups. Within that quote lies another problem for the modern marketer of any product, but especially of such a universally popular star as Beckham. Although everybody likes him and appreciates the same fundamental qualities and

values in him, different groups of people are attracted to –
and want to buy – different aspects of him. Understanding the
different reasons why people buy your product, grouping
similar motivating factors together and identifying the types
of people who share them is something that marketing people
call market segmentation. Indeed, "segment your target
audience" is often known as the first rule of marketing. The
idea is that by understanding how different consumers think,
you can market the same product in different ways to
different people, and so make a lot more money.

So "David Beckham," "Beckham," "Becks" and "DB" can be
used in different ways and at different times to sell different
types of product: Beckham the authentic football name on the
back of shirts, David Beckham the persona on soccer games,
DB on fashion items, Becks as a cheeky nickname on
throwaways such as "Simply the Becks" T-shirts. His various
names not only help him appeal to a wide range of people,
they also help him sell more to them.

Then there are the characteristic Beckham poses. In the
film *Zoolander*, a terrific spoof of the male model industry, the
main character had a trademark pose called The Magnum; in
much the same ,way, Beckham has certain looks that are
merchandised and used for different marketing purposes.
One is the nice boy next door, arms behind back, smiling
Beckham in a soccer shirt that passes the parental
acceptability test and adorns the bedroom walls of a million
lovelorn teenyboppers. Another is the celebrating hero pose
that has been captured many times and turned into posters

that boys love. Yet another is the serious model pose used to best effect in the marketing of Police sunglasses. Still another is the cheeky look used in the Brylcreem ads. And then there's the dedicated, focused, intense professional that gazes out of a thousand posters promoting football or sports products.

Beckham's identity has another dimension: his fashion sense. If his names convey his ordinary, down-to-earth quality, his clothes and hair reveal the sense of style that people associate with him and that forms an important part of his outlook on the world. When we asked people what they associated most with the way David Beckham looks, we got the same answers again and again: "the hair," "that Mohican," "he's always got his hair wonderfully styled," and of course "that sarong," "wearing his wife's panties."

This prompts a few questions. Why does he change fashions and haircuts so often? Why is he so happy to have intimate details about his clothes revealed? Is it just whim, his sense of humour, or a more calculated decision? If it is the latter, who advises him about which look is in: his wife? His management team? Or the sponsors who pay him a lot of money to project their brand and want to ensure he looks right for their image? The answer is probably that Beckham is naturally style-conscious and likes to follow fashion. However, he is also given advice about his look, and changing it often creates more opportunities to sell different images of the same product.

Beckham clearly took an interest in his appearance before he even burst onto the public scene; early photos of the young player feature the classic "footy" haircut of short, blown-back hair with a centre parting. Nothing special about that; but by the time he became a public figure, he had already adopted the floppy hair that was to become part of his brand identity for the next few years, and to which he returns as his quintessential look. There's no reason to assume this look was chosen for its appeal to women or for any calculated marketing reason. It may simply have been serendipity that a man who was very much in touch with his feminine side and naturally understood the importance of his appearance should have chosen a hairstyle that made him look distinctive and highly attractive.

Since we no longer wear hats in the way that people habitually did as late as the 1950s and even early 1960s, hair has become an important way of projecting our personal identity. This is especially true for a footballer, who wears the same strip as his team mates and so has limited opportunities for differentiating himself from them. Footballers' hair has long been subject to comment, but most noteworthy hairstyles, such as sideburns or the mullet, were shared by a number of players. Beckham is one of the few to have set hair fashions so that certain styles are associated with him alone.

Indeed, hair became a defining part of Beckham's brand identity. First to exploit it was Brylcreem, once a byword for hairstyling products: a thick, white, strong-smelling cream that was at the height of its popularity in the 1950s and 1960s. In the 1970s it advertised the "Brylcreem bounce," but it was the "Brylcreem boys" – young, well-groomed, fashion-

conscious working-class men – that entered popular consciousness. By the 1990s, this highly distinctive, down-to-earth British brand had fallen out of favour with a market in which men's grooming and personal care products had become increasingly popular, and in which waxes, gels and other products were putting up stiff competition. Beckham's equally distinctive, down-to-earth personality proved to be a perfect fit with the brand. Sales rocketed by 55 percent in the year he advertised it.

Not only was the floppy hair distinctive and suited to the catwalk as much as the pitch, it was also in tune with the times. The Britpop and boy band eras had just come to an end and longish, slightly unkempt hair was in. Blessed with popstar looks and beamed into millions of houses around the world courtesy of Man Utd, Beckham was idolised and his look copied.

Many people believe that the floppy hair was abandoned after the disastrous sending-off against Argentina, and that Beckham returned bearing the shaven scalp of a penitent monk. In fact, he did not change his hairstyle fundamentally until some time after the birth of his son Brooklyn in 1999, by which stage his rehabilitation was well under way. When Beckham started the 1999–2000 season, it was with a serious shaved haircut that signalled his intention to do the business on the pitch. It also spiked the guns of those who were waiting to use his old image as a way to parody and abuse him. In addition, it marked his rite of passage from single man to husband and father. And it brought his relationship with

Brylcreem to an end. Variations on the shaved look have followed over the years, including the "tramlines" through his skinhead and the AstroTurf look with a subtle centre parting in gelled hair.

The next major tonsorial event was the notorious Mohican. The style had been making something of a fashion comeback: its aggressive sculptured cut and rebellious attitude were in sharp contrast with the soft, wavy look that preceded it. The Mohican did two things for brand Beckham: it created further interest in him as an icon and not just a player, and it established him as his own man with his own sense of style. It also helped balance the husband and father image created by his marriage and the birth of his first child.

Getty Images

As any marketer will tell you, the worse thing a pop star can do in fans' eyes is to get married; it destroys every girl's fantasy of being the one for him. Worse still, it transforms the unattainable hero into an ordinary bloke.

Beckham seemed at the time a happy and doting father as well as a loving husband, but pictures of delighted parents have a short shelf-life: good for an edition or two of *Hello* magazine, but not much more. Being ordinary as a person is no crime, but being boring as a celebrity is a sin. For people to buy new images, Beckham would need a new look that would surprise and intrigue them, be as iconic as his previous floppy hairdo and create a stir to offset the cosiness of his domestic life.

The Mohican had an amazing effect. Thanks to the tremendous exposure that playing for Man Utd brings, the look was soon being copied from Birmingham to Beijing. In Japan, one newspaper called the adoption of the look by female office workers the trend of the year, while the *Sydney Morning Herald* claimed women even adopted the style for their pubic hair. But the Mohican was always going to have a limited life; the initial shock eventually fades and turns to boredom or irritation. It is also incredibly impractical; if you are at school or work, walking around with a Mohican is unlikely to be well received, and once you have it, you are stuck with it.

And so the Mohican passed, and with its passing a new phase in Beckham's career got under way. It is clear that Beckham wanted the England captaincy, and intended holding on to it: "I did not want this as a one-off, I wanted it for good," he says in his biography. As someone who has always taken his responsibilities as a footballer seriously, he was aware that being the England captain gave him a certain status to uphold. The Mohican did not sit well with that image, and he returned to a more conventional hairstyle.

Moreover, the Mohican is such an idiosyncratic style that it limits the types of product and service you can endorse – which is a nuisance if your key strength lies in appealing to just about everyone. This was not a look that all marketers wanted to have associated with their products. So the decision to drop it would again have been motivated by a mixture of football-related and commercial reasons, as well as changing tastes and fashions and his own innate sense of style.

By the time Beckham took England into the FIFA World Cup finals in 2002, he sported a softer tufty look: a universal hairstyle for a global stage. Then, when Romeo was born and he risked looking like a comfortable dad, he adopted a wolfish style: a rough and ready bleached-blond look with matching stubble to sex up his image again. Since then, we've seen the Alice band, the corn braid he wore when meeting Nelson Mandela, and the samurai look (long flowing locks with exaggerated ponytail) he has sported at Real Madrid.

Beckham's hairstyle changes at key moments in his life and, it seems, at points in the season where interest in his look may be flagging. His hair then becomes a way both of keeping the Beckham brand in the news and of continually refreshing its image so that it never becomes predictable or safe. His choice of hairstyle has become increasingly eclectic, even ethnic, in keeping with the rediscovery of tribal imagery and its entry into mainstream fashion trends. Beckham's hair thus serves as further proof of his role as an intermediary between the true trend pioneers and the mass market: by wearing these styles, he confers wider legitimacy on them.

Hair has become so conspicuously associated with Beckham that one woman who claimed to have had an affair with him even referred to the well-groomed hair that in the words of the poet Alexander Pope is "less in sight."

Hair is one aspect of Beckham's identity that is constantly changing; the other is clothes. Beckham's keen fashion sense has always made him a natural for the tabloid front pages – never more so than in 1998, when he was photographed entering a fashionable restaurant wearing a sarong. When, two years later, it became known that he enjoyed wearing his wife's underwear, he was showing that knew how to use clothing provocatively to send signals to the public that he was a different kind of footballer, and a different kind of man. His foray into cross-dressing excited a lot of attention, provoked debate about what was appropriate in fashion and won Beckham some new gay aficionados, as well as establishing his credentials as an early metrosexual. It may also have represented a way of expressing enjoyment of his sensual and sensitive side; certainly, it reflected an increasing androgyny in the fashion choices of both men and women.

Beckham himself attributes the wearing of the sarong and the knickers to his personal sense of style and fun. No doubt that had a role to play, but think about it for a minute: you are a celebrity footballer and people take photos of you wherever you go. You are dressing up to go out to a famous restaurant. Do you choose a) the Italian suit with the silk shirt or b) a traditional Asian skirt now worn by girls at the beach? And if you choose the latter, do you phone people up and ask them what it will do for your image? I suspect a deliberate desire to shock, and not just a passing fashion whim, was at play.

After the 1998 FIFA World Cup debacle, Beckham became more conservative (Posh's knickers apart). Even so, rumour suggests he had a hand in the way the England players dressed and the choice of Armani as tailor for their suits. The ultra-thick knot in his tie and the bag strapped across his chest were further examples of Beckham's seriousness about the management of his image and visual identity. His style is studied, and his commitment to his personal aesthetic is yet another facet of the dedication he shows in every element of his life.

Then there are the tattoos: the latest manifestation of the way Beckham takes a cutting-edge fashion trend and introduces it to the widest possible audience. They show how important it is for him to remain contemporary, and how he takes trends and tweaks them to communicate his values. The choice of a guardian angel over his Romeo and Brooklyn tattoos is not only a fashion trend but a way of stating what is important in his life, and helps establish him as a likeable and down-to-earth guy. According to his Manchester tattooist, 50 more guardian angels have been inscribed on dedicated Beckham fans.

There's another aspect of Beckham's identity that changes, but is based on a constant: the club number on his shirt. For years, his number 7 shirt was the most sought-after Man Utd garment. Indeed, it was so strongly associated with him that he was given it as his England shirt number too, and it became incorporated into a trademark. It's hard to think of any other footballer whose number is so important. When he moved to Real Madrid, there was much speculation as to whether he would keep the same number, but it already belonged to Raul Bravo and – footballers being a superstitious bunch – he wasn't prepared to give it up. Real Madrid was also reluctant to give Beckham the number 7, as it might have suggested that one player was greater than the team.

In the event, it didn't matter. Such was Beckham's appeal that when he was given the number 23 shirt, it instantly became *the* must-have item. Former Real Madrid hero Alfredo di Stefano presented Beckham with the shirt at a ceremony that was beamed live across the world. And people didn't fail to notice that 23 was the number made famous by American basketball legend Michael Jordan.

Marketers have learned that consumers are strangely attracted to numbers. As well as being universally understood signs, they can be seen as cool, technical, mysterious. Levi's has its 501s, BMW its 3 and 5 series and Nokia its 301. The UK has a third-generation mobile operator known simply as 3. Numbers intrigue people and carry cultural significance; seven is considered a lucky number in the west while four is an ill-starred number in some Asian countries, for example.

But what is most interesting about Beckham's 7 shirt is that he inherited a number that was already laden with significance and then proceeded to commandeer it to such an extent that it is difficult to think of anyone else being able to fill it in the same way, at least in the near future.

The number 7 shirt belonged to Cantona, and before that Bryan Robson, and before that George Best, so when Beckham inherited it he was donning a noble mantle. The BBC's website once carried a poll asking who was the greatest all-time wearer of the number 7 shirt. The results of the 3,360 online votes were:

1. George Best (42%)

2. Eric Cantona (39%)

3. David Beckham (10%)

4. Bryan Robson (9%).

Evidently Beckham was regarded as a less distinguished wearer of that shirt than Cantona or Best, but there is no doubt who the world thinks owns that number. Beckham was not the first to recognise its power; Cantona registered the trademark Cantona 7 and used it on a range of products including wine. But he never achieved the same level of association with the number, or shifted so much merchandise.

Beckham benefited from wearing the number 7 shirt at a time when the English premiership had become the most popular and widely broadcast soccer league in the world. Millions of people across the globe watched Beckham once or twice a week for much of the year, and he also benefited from being the first truly commercially minded wearer of the shirt. So everyone saw it as his shirt, and many wanted to buy it.

To sum up, the Beckham identity is a complex arrangement of essential and unchanging elements (his names) and ephemeral and adaptable parts (hair and clothes). These elements are used in a number of ways to communicate brand Beckham. Some, such as his names, reassure us of his essential down-to-earth quality; some, such as his hairstyles, add dimension and personality. By changing elements in the mix, he manages to find new and different ways of establishing a rapport with diverse audiences, and provide fresh material for publicity and merchandising.

GOLDENBALL 4

A celebrity must manage his
or her identity with the same
meticulous attention to detail
and awareness of its impact
as a typical brand. Every look,
every syllable of your name,
every stitch of your clothes and
every follicle of your hair is
part of your brand identity and
needs to be treated with care.

5

THE BECKHAM BRAND IN ACTION

Twenty-three brand-building moments

I was in Massachusetts on a training course during the 1998 World Cup. We all gathered to watch the Columbia match, which England had to win. It was nail-biting stuff. England was 1–0 up through Darren Anderton, and won a free kick outside the area. Up stepped Beckham. "Oh no!" I shouted. "He never scores for England. He'll never get that in. He can't do it at international level." A moment later, I was screaming at the top of my voice, "He did it! He did it!" I turned around and the Harvard professor who was leading the course said with his customary dry wit, "Well, the brand delivered."

Beckham remains a popular figure in our consciousness not just because he looks great or has a famous wife, but because he is a great footballer and has a lot of personal strengths too. It is what he does, not just who he is, that gives him the legitimacy to dominate the newspaper headlines.

Brands have become so strongly identified with packaging and advertising that most people think that is what brands are: an artificial image projected onto an inert product, a packaged soft drink on a shelf or a fancy TV ad for clothes. But recently brand owners have come to realise that what consumers want is an authentic experience, not just a pretty promise. They have seen how brand equity can be undermined or destroyed by a failure to deliver.

Critical to the delivery of the brand experience is the people who actually work for or represent the brand. Separate studies in Europe and America have shown that a startling 66 percent of all customer defections are prompted by an inappropriate attitude on the part of a person representing the brand. Staff (stewards on an airplane, tellers in a bank) are the culprits in most cases, but corporate spokespeople and even celebrities used to promote a brand can be responsible in others.

A brand proves itself by what it does: by the actual value it delivers and by the way it behaves in any situation, spontaneous or planned. This is particularly true of celebrity and professional sports star brands. They earn their right to figure in public consciousness and command fees for appearances through their performance on the screen or pitch. If they fail to deliver, they cease to be relevant. But if they manage themselves astutely, they can extend their commercial life for a long time after their careers are over; think of Elizabeth Taylor, George Foreman and even a minor personality like Vinnie Jones.

So how does brand Beckham shape up in terms of what he delivers? I've chosen 23 moments (numerically significant, of course) from his soccer and celebrity career, and assessed how far they are "on brand." Do they show that the values he embodies, his purpose and his personality have affected his choices, as they would for any good brand? I've given each moment a BILB (*Brand it like Beckham*) score out of 10 to reflect how much the way he handled the event contributed to the building of the Beckham brand.

1. Beckham signs for Man Utd

BILB rating: 10

This is an easy one, but shouldn't be overlooked. His selection by Man Utd and agreement to sign for them shows us the Beckham brand in action at the early age of 16. It was no doubt his dedication to the nurturing of his talent that attracted the scouts and earned him the place. But why choose Man Utd?

In 1991, Man Utd was not the force it is now. It had won a single trophy – the 1990 FA Cup – in the previous five years. The league title had eluded it since the 1960s. Arsenal and Liverpool were the great teams of the time. Didn't Beckham aspire to join them? His decision to join Man Utd, as we saw earlier, demonstrated his sense of style. He had supported the club from childhood because of its entertaining brand of football and the glamorous culture surrounding it. And although it was in the doldrums at the time, the club clearly had the heritage, the potential and the desire to be the best team in the world. What better place for someone who wanted to be the greatest footballer he could?

Though Beckham didn't know it at the time, the arrival of the premiership would give him the biggest possible global distribution channel and promotional medium for his brand.

2. That Wimbledon goal

BILB rating: 10

Instinctive, accurate, visionary and beautifully struck, the goal that launched his career is a wonderful encapsulation of the Beckham brand. Let's not ignore the obvious; it was his dedication to perfecting his shooting and crossing technique on the training ground that gave him the skill to perform that feat. But I would argue that a player who spots an opportunity to score such a theatrical goal has an innate sense of style that finds expression at moments like this.

And then there was the jubilation afterwards: ecstatic and genuine, but also mannered and controlled (it's true that goal scorers rehearse their celebrations). It trademarked the goal, as if he were saying, "I did this, and you can expect more of the same." In marketing, people talk about branding an experience: when customers encounter a great product or service, make sure your logo is there to remind them where it came from. In his moment of triumph, his face up close in camera, Beckham was branding the experience too.

We must also consider the context: a premiership game featured on one of the most popular TV sports programmes. The goal was guaranteed to be shown over and over again. It would get people talking in the pub and at work, and encourage legions of imitators in a thousand parks and back yards up and down the country. What better opportunity to introduce the Beckham brand to a mass market?

3. The Brylcreem deal

BILB rating: 6

Beckham's first major commercial contract played consciously off the image of his hair and his role as a soccer player. The adverts were important in launching Beckham as a brand in his own right, a face that could be recognised off the football pitch. He was an interesting choice for a brand in need of revitalisation: his youth, vigour and style obviously benefited Brylcreem, but it is less clear what such a dated brand could give to Beckham in return. The answers are that a) it was one of the first deals put on the table, and the money was too good to refuse; and b) the brand fitted Beckham's down-to-earth Essex-boy image and made him more accessible as a star.

4. The sarong

BILB rating: 8

Not long before the 1998 FIFA World Cup, Beckham shocked the footballing world by turning up at a restaurant in a sarong. Contrast this with the events of two years earlier: before Euro 96, Gazza and co. had made headlines for binge-drinking in a bar in Hong Kong and trashing a Cathay Airways plane on the way home. Beckham seemed to be consciously setting a different agenda for himself and for footballers in general. With Posh's support, he was clearly making his sense of style an integral part of his brand identity.

This was a smart move in PR terms. He was making the most of his looks and encouraging fashion houses to consider him not just as a footballer but as a style icon. The sarong brought him huge publicity and widened his commercial appeal, even if it also paved the way for some of the vitriol that was to come later.

5. Posh Spice

BILB rating: 10

This marriage made in marketing heaven was also it seems a marriage of hearts and minds. Victoria Adams and David Beckham had much in common, including their Essex upbringing. They were probably the only people who could understand the mad world they were both living in. Beckham's description of their courting days, and how they were refused entry to a Chinese restaurant where all they wanted was a Coke, again reveals that down-to-earth quality admired by many. They chose each other for all the right reasons, and up until David's move to Real Madrid, remained as happy as it is possible to be despite the fishbowl they live in. The fact that Posh did not immediately join Becks in Spain is thought by some to have put the relationship under strain. Allegations about his infidelity are bound to create further pressures. Still, all relationships go through difficult times; the test will be how they cope with it.

Their relationship gave both partners a huge publicity boost and established them as the new royalty among celebrities. Moreover, as we will see later, it gave Beckham a companion who would also be a savvy brand manager.

6. Goal against Columbia

BILB rating: 10

Beckham's first goal for England came at a critical time, in a game the team had to win to stay in the competition. This was also a critical time for Beckham's reputation. He had been left out of the first game against Tunisia, and was brought on only as a substitute against Romania. He had something to prove, and he proved it. Unfazed by all the free kicks he had missed throughout his England career, he pulled it off this time. His dedication and refusal to buckle under pressure paid off. And he must have known he was performing on a global stage from which people would learn more of the phenomenon that is Beckham.

7. Sending-off against Argentina

BILB rating: 0

There was no excuse for this, as Beckham freely admits. Repeatedly fouled by wily opponents, Beckham lost his cool. In front of the referee, legions of England fans and millions of TV viewers, he kicked out and was sent off. But it was rather a feeble kick, almost as if some involuntary spasm of the knee jerked his leg up while he was lying on the ground. He was not the type of player for a full-on fist fight like Roy Keane, or a karate kick like Cantona. There was something slyly stylish about that flick.

In brand-building terms, it could have been a disaster. The incident illustrates how fragile celebrity brands are. One slip, and a reputation is destroyed. Companies that have been queuing up for endorsements will be nowhere to be seen.

8. The comeback

BILB rating: 10

Brand owners often say that a crisis is an opportunity in disguise. If you have spectacularly screwed up and alienated your customers, you have the chance to prove yourself to them in adversity. Studies have shown that customers are actually *more* loyal to companies that have given them a bad experience but then retrieved the situation by apologising, providing unconditional refunds or offering something of greater value than what was lost.

In a sense, this is what Beckham did. His brand could have been dead in the water, but he stayed true to his values and came back determined to provide Man Utd with its best-ever season. The team's achievement of a remarkable treble was in no small part due to his efforts. Brand Beckham proved it was an authentic product, and people soon forgave, if not forgot, that moment of summer madness.

9. Brooklyn Beckham

BILB rating: 10

The birth of his son was evidently one of the happiest days of Beckham's life. The choice of name and the story behind it also made a marvellous PR coup. No one would suggest that the couple were motivated by marketing reasons, but the name Brooklyn is further proof of Beckham's idiosyncratic sense of style and natural flair for creating positive publicity. The timing – so soon after Beckham's sending-off – no doubt helped to win back hearts for him too.

10. The Pepsi deal

BILB rating: 8

The face of a new generation was the ideal spokesman for a brand that claimed to be the choice of a new generation. This was one of Beckham's most lucrative contracts, and ensured that his status as a footballing icon received massive international exposure. Pepsi needed top-class players to counter Coke, which had virtually sewn up football with its official sponsorship of the FIFA World Cup. For Beckham, the deal not only made him a lot of money but also projected him as a sympathetic personality. In one famous ad, Beckham gives a boy his football shirt, only to see him use it to wipe his can of Pepsi. The ad allowed Beckham's self-deprecatory side to show through. When the deal was cut, Beckham was not the worldwide superstar that he is now. Being signed up by his first global brand gave him the opportunity to use its powerful distribution system to introduce himself to an international audience of football fans and non-fans alike.

11. Left out of the Leeds game

BILB rating: 10

Beckham's decision not to turn up for training in March 2000 so that he could look after Brooklyn while Posh went looking for work or shopping (depending on whom you believe) was another defining moment in the building of the Beckham brand. By standing up for his right to be with his family, Beckham set another media agenda. Alex Ferguson might have won the immediate battle by dropping him, but Beckham won the PR war. Ferguson was seen as a bully, and Beckham as a decent guy with the right priorities.

Here is further evidence that Beckham is the symbol of a new generation of players – one that many of the game's old guard find incomprehensible. Missing training because you have been out on a bender the night before is one thing, but missing training because you decided to look after your kid ... ?

12. The OK! wedding

BILB rating: 7

This one depends on your personal taste, I guess. Some saw it as garish ostentation. Among the cream and gold trimmings, Beckham seemed for once to have lost his sense of style. The guest list was studded with stars from sport and showbiz, and was the focus of feverish media interest. But the coverage of the wedding confirmed that Posh and Becks had become celebrities in their own right, independent of the careers that had brought them fame. They became known as the new royal family, and their £2 million home in Hertfordshire was dubbed Beckingham Palace.

The Beckhams chose to turn their wedding into a brand event, a decision that brought them cash, positioned them as true celebrities and broadened interest in them still further. But the extravagance and opulence laid them open to taunts of pretentiousness, and were at odds with David's down-to-earth quality.

13. The England captaincy

BILB rating: 10

This wasn't just a dream come true for Beckham and his management team and sponsors; it also marked the end of his rehabilitation. It's an amazing achievement: within not much more than two years, he went from the country's most vilified player to its most respected. He has conducted himself with the dedication that might be expected of someone determined to hold on to the captaincy. And as team spokesman, he has behaved in the down-to-earth manner we expect of him.

The captaincy conferred a new maturity on Beckham's image. Now he had been given such responsibility, his commercial choices and publicity engagements had to be in keeping with this stature. Thus began the most recent incarnation of the Beckham brand: confident role model.

14. The TV show

BILB rating: 8

There have been several TV documentaries about the Beckhams, but the one that attracted most attention was shown in the UK in 2001. It was a bold but well-judged move for the Beckham brand. David came across as down to earth and dedicated to his family, and looked great throughout. At one point, sitting in the back of a car, he said wistfully, "No one listens to me anyway, 'cause everyone thinks I am stupid" – an artless moment, artfully edited to make us identify with him.

The decision to do the documentary and the way it was presented and edited helped to create a sympathetic and rounded persona for Beckham.

15. The Ali G interview

BILB rating: 7

This could have been a tricky encounter for the Beckham brand. Ali G is a British comedian, a spoof "yoof" presenter with a penchant for embarrassing celebrities who think he is the real thing. Posh and Becks agreed to be interviewed by him as part of the Comic Relief charity telethon. The interview was relentlessly satirical. In one memorable exchange, Ali asked Posh (I paraphrase): "How is the boy? Is he dribbling and beginning to use words?" When she answered "Yes," he leapt in with, "And what about Brooklyn?" Though good-humoured, this could easily have offended a celebrity who was less secure about his image. But Beckham took everything in good part, looked stunning, and probably endeared himself further to the British public.

16. The Rage deal

BILB rating: 5

Here we have a deal that didn't quite work. But it made sense on paper, and showed a deepening understanding on Beckham's (or his advisers') part that he had a valuable image that could be exploited in more sophisticated ways than simply through advertising endorsements. The deal involved Beckham in forming a partnership with games developer Rage to produce a console game, David Beckham Soccer, which enabled players to emulate his football skills. Through this deal, Beckham took the use of his image to another level.

Unfortunately, the product was never as successful as was hoped. The market for football software is intensely competitive, and consumers have huge expectations of the technology. It seems that a product based on a single player couldn't deliver the richness and excitement they demanded. Though the company initially reported a profit surge, it eventually went into liquidation and had to close when no buyer could be found. Even so, the episode shows how Beckham had begun to take control of his brand and push it into new areas.

17. The Greece game

BILB rating: 10

The final qualifier for the 2002 FIFA World Cup was fittingly played at Old Trafford. England were facing the misery of play-offs, and were a goal down with 90 minutes on the clock. As captain, Beckham had been charging around the pitch covering every blade of grass, cajoling every team mate and carving out every opportunity he could for England. Brought down outside the box after a determined run, he stepped up and bent it like Beckham, sending the ball around the wall and into the goal. It was 2–2; England had qualified.

Yet again, he delivered when it mattered: at such a crucial moment that the Beckham brand could only be enhanced.

18. The Police deal

BILB rating: 9

Beckham became the UK face of Italian eyewear designers Police in a £1 million deal. He launched the 2001 collection at a trendy art gallery in central London, and followed through with the next year's collection. The deal was important in being the first commercial contract that didn't draw on Beckham's image as a footballer, but promoted his looks and fashion sense instead. It demonstrated that Beckham didn't need football to appeal commercially to audiences, and reinforced that valuable sense of style. In terms of brand building, it was a clever move.

19. That penalty against Argentina

BILB rating: 10

A recurring theme in Beckham's career is the manifestation of his personal values in a dramatic situation in front of millions of people. This particular occasion featured Diego Simeone and the Argentinians who had knocked England out on penalties four years earlier after Beckham had been sent off. And who should score the winning goal this time? Beckham, from a penalty. His determination to make full amends for 1998 was evident. How could he *not* be the player to take that penalty? And his sense of drama ensured it happened in the most theatrical way.

Once again Beckham was catapulted on to the front pages, and for all the right reasons. As a brand experience, it was phenomenal.

20. The Turkey penalty

This was a truly ridiculous moment in a European championship qualifier in the heat of Istanbul. Beckham stepped up to take a penalty in front of a fiercely hostile crowd, slipped, and ballooned the ball cartoon-style over the bar. The incident showed how resilient the Beckham brand had become since 1998. Instead of becoming the object of ridicule or worse, it was treated with good humour and quickly forgotten thanks to the result: a 0–0 draw that secured England's place in the 2004 championships in Portugal.

Though it couldn't be said that the incident benefited Beckham, the reaction (or rather lack of reaction) to it proved that he now commanded real respect among the press and public.

21. The Real deal

The "Will he, won't he leave Man U?" saga finally ended when Beckham joined Real Madrid in June 2003. A number of clubs would have wanted him, and for a while it seemed he might be on his way to Barcelona. So why Madrid?

For several reasons. First, there is probably no bigger club in Europe in terms of heritage, reputation for style, passion, potential and above all football achievement (nine times European champions, compared with only twice for Man Utd). Second, Real is the best team in Europe at the moment, brimful of legendary stars such as Ronaldo, Figo and Zidane.

Third, it gives Beckham a route to an important global demographic – the Hispanic audience – which could help him eventually in the US. Fourth, because Beckham gave Real Madrid access to the Asian market it coveted, he got a lucrative deal that involved key clauses on image rights.

By choosing Real Madrid, Beckham not only demonstrated yet again what his brand stands for, but also showed that it was being managed for both short-term gain and future value.

22. Focus on football

BILB rating: 8

The decision to focus on football, announced in September 2003, is one of Beckham's smartest moves as manager of his own brand. To be the greatest footballer he can, it is vital that he concentrates on his game at this stage in his career. And even though he has been skilled at managing his brand image so that it can ultimately sustain a life outside football, he must realise that his brand appeal is still underpinned by his performance as a footballer. If anything harms that performance, the value of the Beckham brand will be diminished.

23. Goodbye Tony, hello Simon!

BILB rating: 8

Along with the focus on football came the announcement of a shake-up in Beckham's brand management team. Posh had already asked Simon Fuller, the man who discovered the Spice Girls, to take over the international management of the husband-and-wife Beckham brand. Following much discussion, and after many years with Tony Stephens as agent, Beckham shifted the management of his own career and brand to Fuller's company 19. Harsh though these decisions might appear under the media glare, the fact is that all brands change their management teams when they face new challenges. Now that Beckham is no longer based in the UK and needs to establish himself as a truly global icon, the broader marketing approach of a company like Fuller's is what he needs to give him the best chance of building his brand in the future.

These 23 incidents demonstrate how the Beckham brand responds to events and is shaped by these responses. In virtually every case, Beckham's purpose and values help him take advantage of a situation, rather than merely react to events. When, as in these examples, the situations are dramatic and seen by the widest possible audience, they help to build awareness of and familiarity with the Beckham brand.

GOLDENBALL 5

The best brands set out to do what they say. So it is with personalities as brands. Have a clear goal, stay true to yourself and make sure you get the maximum amount of credit for what you have done.

6

COMMERCIALISING THE BRAND

Don't sell yourself short, and don't sell short-term

"A rose by any other name would smell as sweet"

William Shakespeare

"A hamburger by any other name costs twice the price"

Attributed to Groucho Marx

Beckham has exemplified another trend, and perhaps even been at the vanguard of it. The modern professional footballer needs to know as much about how to cut a deal as how to take a corner; as much about choosing his position in the commercial marketplace as choosing which side of the goal to send his free kick. And as Beckham shows us, he needs to start planning for the long term as early as possible.

One thing we all understand about brands is that they make money. Owning a strong brand is the surest way of generating better profits, charging higher prices and protecting your market share. The same strong brand can be used to sell new and different types of product or to enter new countries. Virgin sells music, air travel, financial services and mobile phones; Disney sells films, theme parks, clothing and toys; Sony sells TVs, stereos, Walkmans, mobile phones and music. Whenever any of them wants to enter a new country, it does so under its existing brand.

As we discussed in the first chapter, brands command this commercial clout because they represent a promise to customers that no other company can match. This promise has less to do with the product and how it is different or better, and more to do with how much I like it or find its image appealing. Marketers put huge efforts into ensuring that the values and image and personality of a brand are right. But just as much thought has to go into how to get it to market: how and where to distribute it, how to promote it, how to price it and how to ensure that once customers have bought it, they keep on doing so.

Successful commercial strategies for brands require:

- **Appropriate distribution:** getting the brand to the right people at the right time and the right place.
- **Effective promotions:** telling people about the brand through appropriate media (everything from the internet to a mailshot), and encouraging them to try it.
- **Sensitive pricing:** ensuring the brand is priced at a level that people can afford, that reflects its desired positioning (luxury goods don't come cheap), and that makes a good margin.

Brand owners also need real flair for what is current and what might be the best way of hooking in to passing trends to ensure the brand stays relevant.

All this is true of celebrity brands, but there are other considerations too. The following golden rules of successful celebrity marketing are attributed to Ron Shapiro, renowned sports agent and author of *The Power of Nice* (I have paraphrased them):[1]

1. Don't overexpose the celebrity brand too early. Don't have too many product endorsements too young.
2. Be selective about what you endorse. You are known by the company you keep.
3. Be quick to spot the right fit. Choose the brand that is going to build you the right image.
4. Don't let commercial deals get in the way of your performance on the field.
5. Don't be a bad boy. Booze, sex and drugs may work for rock stars, but they destroy footballers.

6. Avoid overkill. People (particularly younger audiences) are cynical about hype, so don't over-commercialise.

Nic Couchman, head of leading UK sports law practice Couchman Harrington Associates, puts it like this:

> "The celebrity needs trustworthy advice from people who have his best long-term interest at heart. Finding that is very difficult. Most footballers have little understanding of business and certainly no under-standing of brand building. Why should they? It's not what they have been trained to focus on. The danger for a footballer who suddenly becomes a star is that his management throws every kind of commercial opportunity at him as quickly as possible to get the earn-out before he burns out. The problem is that such over-exposure not only diminishes the player's image, it also leaves him with so many commercial commitments that it can affect his performance on the pitch."

Beckham is rare among players in seeming to have grasped this advice instinctively and at an early age. While still only 16, he appointed an agent to look after his affairs – a precocious act for someone who hadn't even made it into the Man Utd first team, and who in fact was being loaned out to Preston North End. Even more precocious was his choice of agent, Tony Stephens, who at the time was representing established stars such as Alan Shearer. Having an agent meant Beckham could concentrate on improving his game while someone else concentrated on protecting his career.

A further indication of Beckham's early understanding of his commercial affairs is the company he set up in 1996 to handle his financial transactions. The company was called

Footworks, later trading as David Beckham. Arrangements like these are not uncommon for top footballers; they provide a tax-efficient vehicle for managing finances and ensure that money from different income streams is properly tracked. The only unusual aspect is that Beckham set up his company very early in his career, well before major deals started to come in. (Later he and his wife would set up a joint company, Yandella Limited, to manage both their incomes.) Evidently Beckham was good at taking advice on how to manage his assets, something that stood him in good stead when his commercial career took off with the Brylcreem deal in 1997. But before we look at the exploitation of the Beckham brand, it is worth reminding ourselves of the market forces that provided the conditions for the brand to grow.

Most successful brands exist in categories that are expanding or are highly popular. The world likes fizzy drinks, so Coke is able to sell an awful lot of them. Nokia was a little-known Finnish town 20 years ago. It became a worldwide brand not just because it makes outstanding products and markets them superbly, but because it is in a category – personal communications – that has captured public interest and is experiencing massive growth.

Much of the success of David Beckham as a brand comes down to the fact that its product category – football, or more specifically English premiership football – was experiencing a period of unprecedented popularity and worldwide growth. Before the premiership was inaugurated in 1992, football had been in the doldrums, especially in England. Hooliganism, decaying stadiums, defensive playing and a disappointing FIFA World Cup in 1990 had all contributed to its decline. But over the next few years, a number of factors combined to make soccer indisputably the leading global sport, and the English premiership the most watched and talked-about national league:

- FIFA's decision to promote the game globally by ensuring the World Cup would be held in the US and Asia for the first time
- Rule changes introduced by FIFA to encourage a more attacking and attractive game
- The establishment of the European Champions League with its branded approach to promoting European club football
- The rise of cable and satellite television, hungry for content with global appeal
- The emergence and rapid convergence of new communications technologies that allowed rapid, easy and personalised dissemination of information and entertainment, so creating global communities that could receive and respond to images within seconds
- The rise of a new generation of supporters, especially women, who created a demand for a more fashion-conscious game
- In England, the implementation of all-seater, family-friendly stadiums in the wake of the Hillsborough disaster.

The most important thing the English Premiership did in this context was to pool the broadcasting and marketing rights of all the teams competing in the top division, and to establish a single company, EPL, to negotiate the best deals on their behalf. This strengthened teams' bargaining position when negotiating with broadcasters, who were themselves embroiled in a major war between terrestrial (BBC and ITV) and satellite TV channels (Sky and BSB). The money that flowed from these deals, the improvements in marketing and the global distribution introduced by satellite rapidly made the Premiership essential viewing, and transformed football's image.

All this meant that when Beckham played for Man Utd and England, he received global exposure through three main channels that were actively branding themselves to increase their appeal: the English Premiership League, the UEFA Champions League and the international team championships (such as the FIFA World Cup). The figures are startling. Between 1992 and 2002, attendance at English premiership league stadiums increased by over 60 percent as more than 100 million people passed through the turnstiles. Global TV audiences rocketed, with the league being shown in 150 countries to a weekly audience of around 450 million. Fans who attended the matches or watched TV had a seemingly insatiable desire for news, information, highlights packages and merchandise from their favourite teams and players. They had numerous channels to serve their needs: the internet, digital TV, WAP and mobile phones. Global sales of Man Utd merchandise reached an estimated 70 million in

2002. And from 1997 on, many of these sales were of products adorned with the Beckham name and image.

One growth market in particular was Asia. Its consumers are often fascinated by the great icons of the West, be they brands (Coke or McDonald's), film stars, pop stars or footballers. They tend to be early adopters of new trends, and are keen to be part of the global community. Soccer is a passion across much of the continent, but since football teams are still developing at national and club level here, many fans have adopted the great Western players and teams as their heroes. A young footballer with good looks as well as talent represents a potent symbol of success that Asian fans are keen to buy into.

Man Utd has an estimated 17 million fans in Asia – it is the single largest fan base for the club, compared with 11 million in the UK and Ireland – and their appetite for consumption creates a massive market for merchandise emblazoned with their heroes. Beckham is ready-made to appeal to this market in more ways than one. He is softly spoken and appears humble: both important attributes in a culture founded on respect. In fact, he has all the makings of a brand personality that would win hearts from Singapore to Sapporo.

So much for market conditions. Now let's return to the commercial decisions Beckham has made. As each offer came in, he, together with his agents and advisers, had to consider not just the money, but whether the deal fitted with his long-term brand-building ambitions. Anyone building a commercial sports personality brand must address a few specific issues. First, the celebrity needs to be clear about what any endorsement actually covers – precisely what they are and are not lending their image to. This is particularly important for celebrities who may eventually want to create their own branded range of products rather than just endorse other people's.

Another imperative is to be specific about product categories and avoid endorsing too many categories, or competing brands in the same category. By controlling these elements, you can offer more value to the brands that want to use you, and command a premium for exclusivity. At the same time, you protect yourself by not overcommitting. Overcommitment isn't just the risk of having your image splattered over everything or having to attend too many functions; it also means your sponsor might start controlling your life. Rumour has it that when the legendary golfer Gary Player endorsed Californian Sun-In raisins, he was contractually obliged to eat them every day.

Sports personalities will probably need to consider three types of commercial activity:

- **Endorsements:** the most basic and popular option, typically involving adverts, free cars, supermarket openings and autograph signing.
- **Own brands:** a product range that either carries the sports personality's name alone or is co-branded with an established brand.
- **Club-related promotions or merchandising:** a relatively new area in which the sports star agrees a separate financial reward from his club for letting it exploit his name and image in its own promotional activities.

Of these, the own-brand option is potentially the most lucrative. It offers a number of ways of making money, most of which are long term:

- **An upfront fee** for endorsing the product
- **A royalty on sales**
- **A share of the profits**
- **Equity** in the company that produces the goods.

A look at the history of Beckham's deals reveals how astute he has been in exploiting these various commercial arrangements to his long-term as well as short-term advantage, both in cash and in image building.

ENDORSEMENTS

Beckham's first major endorsement deal netted him £1 million for acting as the modern face of the Brylcreem brand. Both sides benefited. Brylcreem saw sales rise by 50 percent by the end of the campaign; Beckham established an image as a fashion icon and not just a footballer. But he clearly wasn't bound by any clauses dictating how to wear his hair, and when he chose to crop it, he was no longer any use as a spokesman for Brylcreem. This must have suited him: Brylcreem was a good launch pad, but hardly the kind of glamorous global brand he would need to hit the big time.

Around the time that Brylcreem signed him, Beckham also began a fruitful relationship with Pepsi. It was an ideal commercial opportunity for him: it paid good money over a period of time (an estimated £3 million in all); it gave him

Getty Images

global distribution (Pepsi was launching an ambush marketing campaign against Coca-Cola's status as FIFA's official partner in world football); and it sat with his mildly rebellious image as one of the new generation of footballers.

One of the features of the use of sports personalities in adverts is that they are no longer just endorsers of product quality; today, they are actors in 30-second big-budget movies. Gone are the days of "Hi, I'm Kevin Keegan. Let me tell you why I use Brut." The Pepsi ads were far more sophisticated. There was the one featuring the young fan who asks for Beckham's shirt only to use it to wipe his Pepsi bottle; the OK Corrall ad where the players find themselves in a penalty shoot-out in the style of a spaghetti Western; and the "Live the Dream" ad involving Sumo wrestling. As well as being designed to intrigue and excite Pepsi's target audience, they transformed perceptions of the personalities they featured from sports professionals to entertainers, thus allowing a skilled celebrity like Beckham to begin building another image for himself. In fact, they function almost like well-paid screen tests, establishing a player's credentials for a trip to Hollywood.

Although the Pepsi contract committed Beckham exclusively within the carbonated soft drinks category and doubtless contained the usual morals clause, it allowed him plenty of freedom to develop his image, which he could then use on this and other products.

Pepsi gave Beckham the global brand he needed, but in a non-core category. The ads earned him good money and helped reinforce his fashionable image, but the big money, as we saw from the George Foreman story, comes from receiving a percentage of sales on your own branded or endorsed items. For that, you need the relevance and credibility to lend a product added value. A Beckham cola would be unlikely to notch up big sales. What he needed was a global sports brand with which he could begin to establish his own co-branded line.

While the search for such a partner continued, Beckham picked up contracts in a range of different categories. Dutch airline KLM used him in a little-known and short-lived deal. Petroleum producer Castrol exploited the concept of performance in a campaign worth £2 million. Japanese confectioner Meiji used him in a campaign so successful that a chocolate statue of him was built in Tokyo.

And then there was the Vodafone deal in which he picked up £2 million for endorsing its products. Within weeks, he had helped shift half a million phones. The company deliberately avoided exploiting him as a football star, concentrating instead on his celebrity status because of its broader appeal: "We use David as a lifestyle icon. He does not appear in our advertising dressed in football kit, he is always appearing in his own casual clothing," Vodafone's corporate communications director, Mike Caldwell, told Reuters. "The great appeal about David is it is universal across the age range. He's liked by children and grandmas and he is liked by football fans and non-football fans."

So Beckham now bestrode a number of categories:

airlines, phones, soft drinks, hair care, chocolate, petroleum. All these deals were useful in earning money and keeping the brand in the public eye, but they remained relatively tactical, and most still traded off his football persona. The next step was to make a deal that would promote him solely as a fashion icon and add to his appeal outside football.

In 2001, Police paid Beckham £1 million to promote its new range of sunglasses in the UK. Naturally, Police secured exclusive rights to Beckham's services in this product category. But what was interesting was the way his image was used. As you might expect, promotions focused on his eyes and face. No reference was made to him as a footballer. This was logical enough; footballers don't as a rule wear sunglasses while playing, so why show them in their kit?

The deal enabled Beckham to take to the catwalk in designer suits, and the posters treated him like a fashion model. He renewed the deal with Police in 2002. So successful was the campaign in the UK, and such was Beckham's growing international fame, that in 2003 he replaced George Clooney as the eyes of Police internationally, in a deal worth £5 million. It was testament to his remarkable ability to make the crossover from sports star to celebrity icon.

OWN BRANDS

On top of the increasingly lucrative endorsements, he began to enjoy growing commercial success with his Beckham-branded product range. If the right deals are made and the products do well, own brands are where the most money can be made and where a sports star can extend his or her commercial life beyond the game.

The first venture into this territory came with the Rage deal. Beckham teamed up with the software company to create a game that would replicate not just his physical image but his particular style of play. This was a new departure in the commercialisation of his brand. He established the principle that not just his name and image, but his movements and techniques – including those famous "bend it like Beckham" free kicks – could be protected and exploited for gain. In March 2004, it was announced that a stylised graphic version of Beckham taking his free kicks

Getty Images

had been created and registered as a trademark, giving him another logo that he could use to create commercial opportunities.

Beckham continued to look for opportunities to associate himself with his own range of products. In 2002, UK retailer Marks and Spencer signed him up to help design and launch a new range of children's clothes under the brand DB07. Beckham owns the DB07 name and must allow M&S to use it under licence. He may earn a fee for designing and endorsing the products *and* a royalty from the sales or a share of profits (perhaps both).

Capturing an exclusive Beckham range was quite a coup for M&S as it struggled to emerge from the doldrums that it was in during the late 1990s. Its image had begun to seem tired and middle-aged, something that Beckham could help to remedy. It also needed to revitalise sales of its children's clothes, which had come under threat from retailers and fashion houses launching junior lines such as Gap Kids. For Beckham, M&S was, like Brylcreem, an interesting choice. M&S isn't Gaultier, and for someone who is such a style icon, it might seem a little infra dig. But the deal was a good fit in other ways. Beckham is down to earth, and so is M&S; he is patriotic, and M&S is British through and through. In commercial terms, too, the venture gave him the opportunity to see how well a David Beckham range could work.

However, the most important development on the own-brand front is the Adidas relationship, which dates back to

1997. By looking at how this relationship has developed, we can understand how the commercialisation of Beckham has changed as his career and his demands have grown.

Like its main rival, Nike, Adidas is extremely professional in its approach to marketing. As a former executive explained: "At Adidas, we were very strategic about whom we would use as a sports endorsement; would they fit with the Adidas brand? Who exactly do they appeal to and why? What is their character like? Would they be likely to do something that might damage the brand? For each personality that we sign, we draw up almost a brand blueprint of the way that person should be marketed; this protects both their image and ours."

Beckham made perfect sense for Adidas. As a dedicated sportsman with natural good looks, but without an aggressive attitude, he was an ideal fit for the professionalism and aesthetics of their brand. It seems likely that Adidas would have had a long-term plan for Beckham when they signed him (one that depended, of course, on how his career developed). To begin with, he mainly took part in advertisements and product endorsements such as the "footballitis" and "I kiss football" campaigns, which featured an elite group of soccer players all of whom were contracted to the company. Beckham was used in particular to promote Adidas's Predator range of boots; their claims of precision and style were well served by a man who could bend a ball into the back of a net from 30 yards out. The contract even ensured that Beckham's family would get a mention, with Brooklyn appearing in a PR piece as the owner of a child-sized pair of Predator boots. (Here was Beckham letting his first sub-brand get some publicity!)

The next stage in the relationship with Adidas was the DB range of clothing, first marketed in the UK. This is probably the most important piece of the commercial jigsaw that Beckham is assembling, in that it allows him not only to earn from an exclusive range but also to build credibility in sports clothing as a brand name in his own right. When the contract with Adidas ends, he will be in a good position to launch a range of his own manufactured by a third party.

Beckham has been paid up to £3 million by Adidas for these various deals. How the relationship will develop in future remains to be seen, but it is becoming clear that Beckham is a vital property for Adidas. His importance is reflected in the way that he has progressed from being one of a number of stars shown together in ads to being the sole or principal figure. It is also rumoured that Adidas was involved in his move to Real Madrid. After all, Real Madrid is an Adidas team, whereas Manchester United was sponsored by arch rival Nike. Think about it: here was Adidas paying Beckham millions to promote its brand, while 450 million people saw him sporting a Nike logo at every match. It was hardly calculated to build the brand image.

CLUB-RELATED MERCHANDISE AND PROMOTIONS

The third element in the commercialisation of the Beckham brand is the exploitation of his image rights in club promotions. This recent development in football marketing is probably the sort of practice that makes Alex Ferguson's blood boil. In essence, players have been getting smarter about their value to a club, and demanding more of the pie. To help you gauge the commercial potential for Beckham at Man Utd, imagine you walk into a shop in Asia and there are two club shirts on sale. One has Gary Neville's name on the back, the other, Beckham's. Which one do you think costs more? Beckham could argue that it isn't Man Utd that is responsible for the price differential, but him, and so he should receive a share of the premium.

Beckham's awareness of his value to the club he represents may have been sharpened by Victoria. Coming from the supremely commercial pop culture, she would be well aware of how easily talent can be exploited by businesses and agents, and how short-lived celebrity can be. It is rumoured that Fergie was irked more by her interference in her husband's contract negotiations than by her distracting lifestyle. Whatever the truth of this, Beckham's last contract with Man Utd, signed in 2000, took so long to complete not because of performance-related pay issues but because of image rights. The eventual deal gave Beckham a total package of £90,000 per week, of which £20,000 was for rights to use his image in club promotions. It wasn't simply a case of Man Utd paying Beckham a fee for the right to use his name; rather, the contract offers him compensation to prevent him challenging the use of his name or image by Man Utd (presumably in perpetuity).

This might sound like a lawyer's distinction, but it was important in commercial terms because it gave Man Utd freedom to distribute images of Beckham anywhere and at any time. The good news for Beckham was that there was no commercial reciprocity, in that the contract allowed him to make as much money as he wanted from outside interests as long as he did not exceed a fixed number of commercial days (those days that a club allows a player to spend on his own commercial interests – sponsorship, advertising and so on – rather than on training, playing or representing the club). The deal marked a recognition that he brought money to his club above and beyond the contribution he made through his playing ability.

The same principle operated in the deal with Real Madrid, but with a difference. Real Madrid pays Beckham a salary that includes an allowance for image rights, but it also receives 50 percent of any fees that he earns from any commercial contracts signed after joining the club. His existing deals with Pepsi and Adidas are not thought to be affected.

Such an arrangement is standard practice for Real Madrid, as well as a good commercial move. Real's sporting director Jorge Valdano revealed that he had discussed image rights at length with Beckham. "It was the key to the negotiations," he said. "We demand 50 percent of our players' image rights. We consider this issue indispensable because the other players have followed this policy." [2] The issue was more complex with Beckham because his image is so powerful, but he agreed. "This agreement marked the player's wish to come to Real Madrid even by losing money. His personal publicity is 111 hours per year and he manages to do this during his holidays."

Estimates of how much Beckham will make for Real, for Adidas and for himself out of the deal vary, but the precise figure is less important than the principle he has established of knowing how to negotiate his brand value with his employer. Beckham enjoys great brand recognition worldwide. "Bekkanu," the Japanese equivalent of "Becks," has 99 percent prompted recognition in Japan, for instance. Experts reckon that around four or five million Asian Man Utd fans will defect to Real Madrid within two years as a result of his transfer. Beckham has done well out of his commercial activities to date, making around £12.5 million a year from endorsements and other marketing deals.

Even so, he lags behind other top sports performers such as Michael Jordan and Andre Agassi. In fact, the world's top sports earners are Michael Schumacher, who makes around £40 million a year for his endorsements, and Tiger Woods, who earns about £35 million a year for his, including some £25 million from Nike. Why does Beckham lag behind? There are probably several reasons:

- Surprising though it might sound, money is not Beckham's chief consideration. His main purpose in life at the moment is to excel as a footballer. Moreover, as a club player – unlike, say, a golfer or a tennis champion – he has commitments that make big demands on his time, so he has fewer commercial days to spare than athletes in other sports.

- He doesn't operate in the most lucrative sports market in the world, the US, where the deals are bigger and the rewards greater.
- Whereas Agassi, Woods and Jordan dominate the image of their sports worldwide, Beckham lacks their magic. Though an excellent player, he is no Pele or Maradona.
- He stuck for a long time with a British football agent as his principal commercial adviser rather than going to one of the big talent marketing groups.

Some people might imagine that being a celebrity gives you a licence to print money, and in a sense it does, but commercialising a celebrity brand is no easy task. It calls for marketing skills, legal knowledge and an awareness of the importance of long-term image building. This is why the top brands in sport are managed by companies that understand what makes a great talent *and* what makes a great brand. Beckham has shown by the way he has allowed the commercial exploitation of his brand to develop that he understands all the key principles of branding. He demonstrates a marketing nous that enables him instinctively to make or to accept decisions that generate cash and build image. In that respect, he may not be unique as a sportsman, but he is rare among football players.

GOLDENBALL 6

Commercialising a personality brand requires you to think not only about how much you can earn right now, but also about how any deal is going to help you achieve your brand goals and sustain your revenues in the long term.

Notes

1 See *www.bizjournals.com*
2 *www.espnsports.com*

7

CO-
BRANDING

Choose your partners with care

A man is known by the company he keeps.

Proverb

Another aspect of the building and commercialisation of the Beckham brand deserves a closer look. When Beckham appears in association with other brands, what role do they play in helping to shape his own brand image? What strengths and qualities does he draw from them? How does he make their attributes his own? Here I am thinking not of commercial brands such as Adidas and Pepsi, which as we have seen bring synergies in terms of brand image and commercial opportunities, but of Man Utd, the England football team, Real Madrid and Victoria Beckham.

In marketing, the alliance formed by two separate brands owned by different companies to bring a single product or service to consumers is called co-branding. (It is not to be confused with sub-branding, in which one brand creates or buys another and endorses it; in such cases a single company owns all the brands, as Nestlé does with KitKat and Nescafé, for instance.)

Co-branding can take a number of forms, including:

- **Ingredient branding**, such as Compaq or IBM computers with "Intel Inside." Here the house brand benefits from the special ingredient and the ingredient brand benefits from the rest of the product mix.
- **Joint-venture branding**, such as Sony Ericsson phones. Here two different parties bring equal and complementary strengths to create a product range.
- **Alliance branding**, such as the oneworld airline alliance involving BA, American Airlines, Qantas and

others. Here two or more brands form a partnership to provide a seamless service.

As we will see, most of Beckham's co-branding is of the ingredient or joint-venture kind. By entering a co-branding arrangement, a brand is acknowledging that it can provide only so much of what a customer wants, and needs another brand or brands to fill the gap. Each brand gains access by proximity to the other's competence and image, and in time may even acquire the other's values by association in consumers' minds.

For sports celebrities, co-branding works in similar but less orchestrated ways:

- Major tennis or golf tournaments often rely on the presence of a top player for their interest and appeal; what would Wimbledon be without Tim Henman (apart from less emotionally gut-wrenching for the British audience)? Similarly, clubs have star players who become major attractions. Both can be seen as examples of ingredient branding.

- Clubs or tournaments often co-promote with a celebrity, especially after he or she has stopped playing, as with the Gary Player Classic golfing tournament. This is an example of joint-venture branding.

- When two or more celebrities get together and offer something unique, the result can be described as alliance branding. This is more common in individual sports such as golf or tennis, where a tournament promoter can't rely on a single big name to attract a crowd but needs a number of well-known players. In effect, the English Premiership League is an alliance brand: its guarantee of top-drawer entertainment depends on the promises of its member brands (clubs including Man U, Liverpool and Arsenal), most of which are better known and have been established for longer than the league itself

For soccer players in particular to make it big as brands, they need the co-brand of a major club. Kevin Keegan may have been a great player at Scunthorpe, but he needed Liverpool to endorse and promote him. Paul Gascoigne may have been a talent at Newcastle, but he needed the move to Spurs and then to Lazio to raise his profile.

MAN UTD WITH ADDED DAVID BECKHAM

Let's consider the Beckham brand in the light of all this. First comes its role as ingredient in the Manchester United team. Man Utd is the big brand that effectively launched Beckham to the world. He derived much of his credibility and almost all of his global publicity opportunities from its endorsement. Its fan base is vast: 11 million in the UK and Ireland, 17 million in Asia, 9 million in Europe, 12 million in the Americas. With its matches beamed to 450 million viewers a week, its reach is exceptional too. Then there are the financial opportunities that the club opens up, and last of all its brand image: a strong tradition of stylish football.

As far as Man Utd was concerned, Beckham was more like one of its sub-brands than a co-brand. Beckham merchandise was among the club's most popular lines, and something it exploited to the hilt. Of all shirt sales worldwide, more than 50 percent were Beckham's number 7. Added to that were the numerous magazines, posters, products, website features and MUTV programmes that led with his image; no wonder he got an extra £20,000 a week to make sure he didn't complain.

Man Utd has a policy that no one player should receive more publicity than any other. When it initiates promotion, sponsorship or publicity opportunities, it operates what it calls a three-player rule: that is, there must be at least three players present so that it is the team that benefits and not an individual player. But it is hard to see this rule at work in the way the club featured Beckham. His fame was in the end something of a double-edged sword. Not only were they exploiting an asset, they were building a brand that ultimately belonged to someone else and might depart at any time, taking its revenue streams with it – which is what happened in the end. Still, Man Utd is a bigger and longer-established brand than Beckham, and will find new heroes to nurture. For his part, Beckham managed the co-branding relationship well, extracting maximum exposure and commercial gain while building an independent reputation.

Getty Images

POSH AND BECKS: THE JOINT VENTURE

The next co-branding relationship is one of the most high-profile joint-venture brands ever in the world of entertainment: Posh and Becks. Beckham arrived on the scene just as the popularity of the Spice Girls was beginning to wane. The publicity gave Posh's career a massive boost and marked the first major stage in Beckham's journey to celebrity status. It's worth reminding ourselves how big they were when they met. At the time, Posh probably had a more valuable brand than Becks. She was certainly worth a lot more: at 25, her estimated value was £25.5 million. Her future husband was 24, and worth a mere £7 million.

Setting aside the personal and emotional side of their relationship, let's look at how they have managed its public side, and particularly how they have developed their co-branding. The Posh brand brought a number of things to Becks that he needed to broaden his appeal. First, she gave him access to the entertainment world and the tabloid press, increasing his media coverage. He had been given the front-page treatment before, but only sporadically. With Posh on his arm, coverage was virtually guaranteed. Next, she gave him added human interest and an extra dimension to his personality. And after they married and she took his name, she gave him another way of propagating the Beckham brand name.

Victoria also gave him something else that he probably needed, and that has become more apparent over the years: a greater focus and discipline in building the Beckham brand. In short, she brought him dedicated brand management. Her experience as a Spice Girl and later as a solo performer exposed her at a young age to the commercial realities of the entertainment world. That experience, coupled with her innate street savvy, was to prove vital in managing her husband's and her own career.

It is no coincidence that after his marriage to Posh – and particularly after her own career stalled in the wake of disappointing sales of her solo album – Beckham's commercial deals and career management became sharper and more focused. As one insider said: "There is no doubt that Victoria's influence in the relationship is that she provides the strong commercial head; she not only loves him, she also recognises how much he can be worth if he makes the right decisions, and is determined to ensure that he does." She doubtless understood early on that the Beckham brand had the potential to eclipse her own.

The first sign of Victoria's hard-headed commercial nous came just days after Beckham's image was tarnished by the sending-off against Argentina in 1998. She and her mother Jackie became directors of a company known as Yandella Limited. It was described as a general commercial company, but on 1 March 1999 its true purpose was revealed when David Beckham became its third director. Clearly, the company had been created to maximise earnings from the future joint business activities of the new king and queen of celebrities. Among the first revenues was the £2.5 million paid by TV production company Planet 24 to film the run-up to their wedding in 1999.

Yandella is the family business. Its name carries no significance; it was an existing company bought off the shelf. Of greater interest is the role of Jackie Adams as director and company secretary; in theory, it gave the Adams family a two-to-one majority at board meetings. Yandella exists to provide a foundation for future ventures selling the Beckham brand name. David has a string of contracts that more than treble his £1.3 million a year on-field earnings, but he is still far from fully exploiting his global fame. He can be expected to have both a longer career and greater earning power than his wife. By setting up Yandella, Victoria was trying to ensure that no deal is overlooked or opportunity neglected.

Victoria's control of the commercial side of the Beckham brand can be seen in the decision to appoint Simon Fuller to handle its global development. Clearly she felt that Tony Stephens could take Beckham only so far, and a change in strategy was needed. "We are going to build a global lifestyle brand focusing on fashion, media and entertainment," proclaimed Fuller. It's hard to imagine a British football agent talking like that. David wanted to retain Stephens alongside Fuller, but ultimately the contractual relationship between Stephens, his other clients and SFX made that impossible, and so Fuller's company, 19, now manages both the joint and the David Beckham brand.

But Posh's influence is not confined to commercial strategy; she also has a lot of control over her husband's brand identity. In a recent TV documentary, his tattooist claimed that she personally supervised the designs for his tattoos, approving the representation of "07" as "VII," for instance. She also seems to exercise power of veto; referring to a proposed tattoo of Jesus standing like Michelangelo's *David*, she reportedly said: "If you have that on your arm and you wear a t-shirt, the feet will be sticking out and look bloody silly." Many husbands would freely admit that their wives choose their clothes and make sure they look acceptable in public. But if I turn up at a party wearing the wrong tie, only one or two of my friends are going to notice or care, whereas for Beckham, every sartorial choice and grooming decision is pored over by millions of people, and a bad hair day can sully his reputation. Though Posh is sometimes accused of being overbearing and obsessed with her husband's image, she is in fact acting like any good "logo cop," ensuring every element of his identity works in his favour.

The commercial potential of the Posh and Becks co-branding alliance is phenomenal. In 2003, they undertook promotional tours of Japan and South-East Asia. Their appearances, endorsements and other activities earned them an estimated £6 million (US$10million) in total. There is no way that either of them could have generated so much interest or income on their own.

They have clearly seen the potential in their co-branding. Tokyo Beauty Centre paid them an estimated £2.2 million to feature in adverts promoting their lifestyle and looks. Since the adverts were shot in Lancashire, they didn't even have to venture far from home. The couple have taken part in several fashion shoots in celebrity and lifestyle magazines. In most of their public appearances, they are inseparable. Every interview, whether it be with Parkinson or Ali G, is conducted with the two of them, and let's not forget the notorious and much lampooned documentary in which they let cameras into their life.

Then there was the management of the publicity surrounding the births and names of their two children. Calling their first son Brooklyn after the New York district where he was allegedly conceived was further proof of their media savvy. When Victoria's second pregnancy was announced, the resulting frenzy of speculation about the sex and name of the child kept the Beckhams on the front pages for weeks. Misleading reports that the child would be a girl and named Paris, again after the place of conception, were allowed to circulate without correction. When a boy finally arrived and was called Romeo, the anticlimax was almost palpable. All the same, the Beckham brand got another boost as David was again revealed as a doting father. And the UK press were filled for weeks with discussions about the merits of Romeo, another iconic name.

The Beckhams seem to accept that it will be impossible for their children to escape public attention. They probably reason that by giving the press a few controlled photo opportunities, they will discourage intrusive paparazzi shots. No doubt they also appreciate that their children make them appear more normal, human and caring, and hence more attractive to a wider public.

Getty Images

The Beckham's co-branding strategy benefited them even when they were promoting their separate careers in pop and football, as the following extracts from the website www.allmovieportal.com suggests:

"Victoria is desperately bidding to spark more interest in her pop comeback, by enlisting the musical talents of her soccer superstar husband David Beckham – A voicemail message left by Beckham in which he tells Victoria he loves her and asks her to call him back was sampled on one of her new tracks."

"David and Victoria Beckham have caused shockwaves with their sexiest photos ever for an Italian style magazine – Beckham, wearing black nail polish and a bondage-style wrist band, is straddled by Adams, who wears a tiny silver dress in the picture for the cover of July's *L'Uomo Vogue*."

Think of Posh and you think of Becks; think of Becks and

you think of Posh. Some argue that Becks got the better deal: he comes over as the modest and likeable one of the couple, whereas Posh grates. It's true that during the allegations of his infidelities in April 2004, there seemed to be something of an anti-Posh undertone: a feeling that if the allegations were true, then she was as much to blame as he was. But this is beside the point. They are promoting the joint Beckham brand that benefits them both. If one suffers in the short term but they both gain in the long term, so what? And consider this: given her head for commercial management, it may be that Victoria will ultimately find her perfect role as principal brand manager of David Beckham™.

To be sure, the Beckham brand does sometimes seem over-exposed. Even in the focus groups we conducted, which were generally highly positive, there were adverse comments about Beckham as a "money machine," and concerns about how long he can stay focused on football. There must always be a risk of consumer exhaustion, where the public get so tired of the Beckham name that they switch off.

Whatever the downside, this particular form of co-branding has brought enormous upside for Beckham. It has broadened his media access and provided new platforms for his image; it has enriched his personality; and it has enhanced his earning power. Let's not forget it keeps him in the public eye too, even during a spell of bad publicity (unless we agree with the saying "No publicity is bad publicity"). And why don't we take him at his word and accept that it has also given him a wife and kids that he adores?

BECKHAM FOR ENGLAND

Two other co-brands deserve our attention. The first is Beckham and the England team.

Beckham's debut at the start of the 1996 season, though reportedly thought premature by Alex Ferguson, conferred authority on him and acknowledged his status as a player of true quality. The sending-off in the Argentina match could easily have destroyed all the positive equity that had been built up in the Beckham brand, but his subsequent captaincy renewed his legitimacy as a great national player, and his performances have won over many of his critics. At the same time, the "three lions" imagery and emotion surrounding the England brand have been transferred to him.

The most interesting thing about this co-branding arrangement, though, is that Beckham gains no direct commercial benefit from it. He receives neither a salary for playing nor any share of the image rights when he appears in promotions. All the money that the Football Association, a not-for-profit organisation, makes from sales of kit, sponsorship, and broadcasting and merchandising rights goes back to the FA for distribution throughout the game. The players get nothing. But the kudos that goes with playing for England naturally adds to their value when they sign contracts with clubs and commercial bodies. Undoubtedly, the drama that has attended Beckham's England career has greatly enhanced his brand value.

BECKHAM GETS REAL

And so to the latest of the co-brands: Real Madrid. With Barcelona vying with Madrid for Beckham's signature, this was the most talked-about deal of 2003. Eventually David opted for Real, £23 million and the number 23 shirt. What does the Real Madrid brand bring that Beckham doesn't have already? First, it ensures Beckham a place in the premier showcase for international talent, which Barcelona couldn't guarantee. Second, Real's legendary stature as the most successful club in Europe complements his own brand image. Third, it establishes Beckham in the international sphere. Fourth, the deal puts him into a team that is sponsored by Adidas and so makes him more valuable to them.

Russel Wong Photography

Most important of all, playing for Real gives Beckham access to the huge Hispanic market. There are over 425 million Spanish speakers in the world, making them the fourth-largest linguistic group after Chinese, English and Hindustani. Every match he plays for Real Madrid gets Beckham's name and image transmitted into millions of Hispanic homes across the globe. This is an important step in building his brand in new markets, particularly the US – the one big market Beckham has yet to capture, and where much money is to be made.

Plenty of commercial opportunities will no doubt flow from the move to Real Madrid, but it is unlikely that it was prompted by short-term financial gain. Beckham may even have taken a pay cut. At Man Utd, he was earning an estimated £90,000 a week (although £20,000 of that was a sweetener for the image rights); at Real, he is thought to make about 6 million euros a year, which works out at just under £80,000 a week. On top of that, he has to give Real 50 percent of any income he earns from new commercial deals. Any short-term gains or losses are clearly less important than the long-term benefits the move will bring.

We can see that Beckham has a clear strategy for choosing his co-brands, and that he manages them to achieve not just maximum revenue, but optimum image transfer – the most important benefit that co-branding can bring.

GOLDENBALL 7

Managing relationships with clubs, other celebrities and even national teams is all part of brand building. You have to choose your partners with care, and manage them with even more care.

8

PROTECTING
THE BRAND

Attack is the best form of defence

"As a celebrity brand all you have is your reputation, your brand; you do not have anything else. You have to understand and protect that intellectual property, because if you don't, everyone will take advantage of it."

Nic Couchman, Couchman Harrington Associates, sports and image rights law firm

Beckham is a legend, and legends sell. So people will want to cash in on that legend even if they have no legal right to do so. Beckham knows that, and he is determined to protect the rights in his reputation that he has built up through his own efforts.

There is a simple fact about owning a brand. If you don't have a trademark, you don't have a brand in any real sense of the word. And if you don't protect your brand as a legal entity and as your intellectual property with the same vigour that you would protect any other property (your home, your car, your jewellery) from abuse or theft, you may even forfeit your rights over it. Sony lost its exclusive legal right to the Walkman name as its proprietary trademark in Australia because it allowed the name to be used by consumers as a generic term for all personal stereos. Sellotape, escalator and Hoover all started out as trademarks but then lost their proprietorial status, although Hoover has fought to get it back again.

The legal protection of brands is often overlooked by marketers, but at their peril. If you do not enforce your legal rights, you can be copied by competitors and even lose your trademark. We should also remember that trademarks and other intellectual property rights exist to protect consumers as well as companies. Unscrupulous traders who copy or steal a competitor's trademark or image are cheating the public and fraudulently passing off one product as another. The repercussions can be grave: for example, a trademarked food product may carry guarantees of hygiene, quality and authenticity that copycat products made from different ingredients and by different manufacturing processes cannot match.

Great brand companies take the protection of their brand image very seriously indeed. They don't just use lawyers to send out warnings or "cease and desist" letters to anyone who infringes their intellectual property. They actively investigate the ways in which their brand could be unfairly or illegally exploited by others. Such companies even hire people to go around asking retailers for their own brands. If these people are given a substitute without being told about it, the companies can threaten legal action for misrepresentation of goods. That's why, if you ask in a restaurant for a Coke and they don't have one, the waiter may ask if a Pepsi is OK, fearing that you work under cover for Coca-Cola and are poised to sue!

There are two aspects to protecting your brand rights:

1. Ensure you have the legal rights in the first place (by registering your name and logo as a trademark).
2. Act to ensure that these rights remain in force (by not allowing your image to be used inappropriately by others or within your own organisation).

In an age of global brands, there has been increasing international harmonisation of intellectual property and trademark law to ensure that companies can enforce their brand rights consistently around the world.

For celebrities, the issue of legal protection of their brand or image is just as important, but even more complicated.

This is because the laws on image rights are not harmonised internationally, and in some countries, especially the UK, they are not particularly clear.

There are three basic types of legal protection open to sports celebrities.

CONTRACTUAL AND INTELLECTUAL PROPERTY RIGHTS

Nic Couchman, a leading sports rights lawyer, explains a player's intellectual property and contractual rights as follows:

> Every player/athlete has a name (e.g. Eric Cantona), facial and other physical or style characteristics and a signature (bushy eyebrows, unshaven appearance, raised collar, runs with a straight back). Players sometimes also have nicknames, logos and associated slogans or even catchphrases ("Oohh ahh, Cantona"). They will also have biographical information and statistical data. All of these elements are referred to as "player indicia" (a legal expression which basically means that these are the elements which are particular to and indicate a specific player and no other).

> Every player/athlete has the ability proactively to lend his support to a commercial entity, whether a sponsor (Nike), an advertiser (Eurostar), a club (Manchester United) or a federation, and as part of such an arrangement to lend (or license) the use of various player indicia. The licensee then has the contractual right to use such indicia – a contractual "image right." If this contractual image right is exclusive to the licensee, the player will not be able to license the same rights elsewhere, depending on the terms of the contract.

PROTECTION AGAINST PASSING OFF

The law in the UK and elsewhere also provides a degree of protection for sports stars and other celebrities through the concept of "passing off." Passing off occurs when an individual or a company seeks commercial gain by falsely representing or implying that a celebrity endorses or supports a particular product or service. For example, racing driver Eddie Irvine successfully sued Talksport (formerly Talk Radio) after it released promotional materials featuring a doctored photo that made it look as though he was listening to a radio bearing the words "Talk Radio." The court found that Talksport had falsely suggested that Irvine was endorsing its station. He was awarded £25,000 in damages – roughly what it would have cost the broadcaster to have secured Irvine's endorsement legitimately.

TRADEMARKS

It is also possible in certain circumstances to register player indicia as trademarks, internet domain names and internet keywords. Registering nicknames and logos as trademarks is likely to be easier than registering names. David Beckham, for example, has filed a European Community trademark application for his full name and other names in a range of trademark classes covering such products as sunglasses, bags, football shirts and hair products.

In addition to these three categories, there are other rules of law – libel, trade descriptions legislation, advertising codes – that can also be called on by a celebrity whose name is being exploited without consent. It is even possible that the European human rights convention, which contains a right of privacy, could be invoked to protect personality or image misuse.[1]

The potential earnings from the image rights of top sports personalities is huge. For example, Real Madrid, which signed Zinedine Zidane for £45.8 million in 2001, could earn £11 million from sales of half a million or so replica shirts bearing his name. It is hardly surprising that celebrities and sports stars have successfully sued for unauthorised commercial uses of their names and images. Notable cases cited by Couchman Harrington include:

- Andre Agassi's pending suit in the courts of Nevada against Rolex for unauthorised use of his image in advertising
- Tiger Woods' suit against a painter who sold portraits of him
- Boxer Muhammad Ali's suit against Playgirl, Inc.
- Mario Andretti's suit against Rolex
- Cricketer Ian Botham's threatened court action against Diageo for use of footage of him in action in the 1981 Ashes Series
- Kieran Perkins' successful suit against a telecommunications company that used a photograph of the champion swimmer in advertising without consent

- Eric Cantona's award of damages in a French court for the unauthorised use of his image on the cover of a video
- The athlete David Bedford's successful complaint under the UK ITC Code against The Number advertising agency for caricaturing him in television advertisements.

As I write this book, an action is being brought in the Belgian courts by a group of Romanian football stars including the legendary Gheorghe Hagi who claim that the use of their names and images in computer games infringes their legal rights. If the action is successful, it will have a huge impact on the developers and publishers of computer and interactive sports games, which until now have been using sports stars' names and images without obtaining licences and permissions from them individually.

So what has David Beckham done to protect his brand? As we shall see from the examples below, he doesn't take protection lightly.

On the contractual rights front, Beckham set up a company called Footwork through which all his rights (and presumably the monies from them) would be managed. He has been highly astute, or at least well advised, on what these rights should cover. As we have seen, his contract with Manchester United granted the club permission to exploit his image for an extra £20,000 a week on top of his player's salary, but only within carefully controlled limits. The contract contained as many as 40 separate clauses relating to image rights.

BECKHAM AND PASSING OFF

This is a notoriously tricky area, but Beckham has shown that he and his management team will not allow any abuses to go unchallenged. Take the case of German beer brand Beck's. In 2001, it ran an advertising campaign featuring a photo of a bottle of Beck's together with a topical word or phrase. In October of that year, following the England v. Greece FIFA World Cup qualifying match in which Beckham scored a last-minute winner from a free kick, Beck's ran an ad bearing the word "Saviour." It was clearly a reference to the other Becks. Though it wasn't derogatory or defamatory, Beck's agreed to pay a donation to charity rather than run the risk of having Beckham complain about its implicit use of his endorsement in the advert.

This example is important not so much in itself but for what it reveals about Beckham's attitude towards protecting his legal rights. After all, it was a minor incident, and if the company had wanted to argue its corner, Beckham might have had trouble proving that it was directly passing itself off as having his personal endorsement. In the event, though, the affair sent a strong signal to the marketing and media world that Beckham would strenuously resist any unfair or unauthorised attempt to profit from his reputation. Such vigilance can itself act as a deterrent against passing off.

BECKHAM AND TRADEMARK

Beckham has registered a portfolio of trademarks including Beckham 7, Beckham 23 and DB07, as well as a graphic representation of his characteristic free kick. A registered trademark is the most powerful piece of intellectual property anyone can own.

There is an important difference between a trademark that has been registered and so is entitled to use the ® sign, and an unregistered trademark that can use only the ™ sign. By virtue of having been registered, the former can prevent anyone else using the same or a similar trademark for the same or similar products or services. If you haven't had your trademark registered – and some trademarks can't be registered because they are too descriptive of a product, like Soft Soap – then you have to use other forms of protection to support a claim of infringement. Because Coke is a registered trademark, it doesn't need to provide evidence that a beverage called Cobe, say, is trying to pass itself off or borrow Coke's image. All it would need to do is tell Cobe that it is infringing a registered trademark, and Cobe would have to stop.

Since the international harmonisation of trademark laws, every country's trademark register features 42 different classes, each covering a different category of goods: class 3 covers perfumes and cosmetics and class 9 covers telecommunication products, for instance. The system allows the same brand name to be used by different companies for different categories of goods that are not in competition with one another. So Nestlé own the name Polo for confectionery, but Ralph Lauren owns it for fashion and Volkswagen for cars. The logic is that consumers would never be deceived into buying a car when all they intended to buy was a packet of mints, so these trademarks can happily coexist.

Beckham's ambition for his brand is reflected not only in the number of different brand names he possesses, but also in the number of categories or classes he has registered. The table below lists some of the major trademarks.

Some of Beckham's registered trademarks

Correct as at 15 December 2003

Trademarks	Status	Classes
Beckham	Registered*	03: Cosmetics and cleaning preparations 06: Metal goods 09: Electronic and scientific apparatus 14: Jewellery 16: Paper goods and printed matter 18: Leather goods 25: Clothing 28: Toys and sporting goods
Beckham 7	Registered	As above
David Beckham	Registered	As above
Beckham	Examined†	29: Meats and processed foods 30: Staple foods 32: Light beverages 33: Wines and spirits
Beckham 23	Examined	25: Clothing

* A valid registration
† An application that has been examined but not yet prepared for publication (the public notification of the intent to register the mark, which allows any third party to object)

From this list, we can see that Beckham has ambitions to sell clothing, food, alcoholic and soft drinks, and even jewellery. Some people may find it amusing that Beckham has a registration for scientific apparatus too – but then his free kicks do defy the laws of physics!

Given the legal minefield surrounding the commercialisation of image rights, it is no wonder that Beckham has been persuaded to use new management (Simon Fuller and 19) to look after his brand. There are many issues to consider when you are trying to get the best deal for your brand, and you can be sure that commercial partners such as Adidas and Pepsi are extremely clued up about how to get the maximum value out of any deal. Nic Couchman puts it well: "You can bet that as far as the deal that Beckham has with Adidas goes, Adidas would have ensured that they got his image rights tied up for the longest period possible and for the widest amount of products and opportunities as possible and for as little as possible."

When Beckham is negotiating his next contract, he will have to consider the following elements to ensure his image rights are protected and he generates maximum value from the deal:

- How many countries is the deal for? "Across Europe" is too vague, for instance; the contract needs to specify the individual countries involved, with a separate fee for image rights in each one.
- What exactly is the contract to cover? This should be defined in detail. "Football shoes" is not precise

enough; the contract should specify a particular line of shoe (such as Adidas's Predator range). Any other line would then need to be covered in a separate contract, subject to an additional fee.

- What is the time period? If a sponsor wanted to tie Beckham up for three years, he shouldn't simply agree a flat fee but should build in an estimate of how the value of the deal should increase year after year.
- Who owns which pieces of intellectual property? If Beckham is being asked to promote an individually branded range such as DB for Adidas, he must make sure that he and not Adidas owns the trademark DB.

"Structuring the contract thoroughly and carefully is vital," says Couchman. "You have got to get the levels of exclusivity correct, the categories right and the commercial rights plan fixed."

For Beckham, the potential is enormous. There are probably at least 30 countries where he is a household name, and a similar number of product categories he could put his name to. If you work it out on a country and category basis, there are probably close to a thousand separate deals that could be done, each with its own value. It is usually only by breaking the deals down in this way that you can maximise value and ensure protection. But this has to be balanced against the benefits of having a smaller cluster of larger sponsors who have global rights. Sport is international and brands are international, and if international brands want to be associated with international sports stars, they will have to pay what it takes.

Protection will continue to be a big issue for the Beckham brand in future, especially now that the internet has opened up new opportunities for commercial piracy. If you type "Beckham" into a search engine, you will find millions of entries. You can be sure that some of them will be unauthorised sites selling images or unofficial or counterfeit memorabilia. By using special "spidering" techniques, a service provided by specialist companies on the web, it is possible for Beckham's managers and lawyers to track down references linked to sites that are illicitly making money from the Beckham brand, and close them down.

Another issue is how to enforce Beckham's rights when he is present in so many countries. The key lies in what Couchman describes as "forum shopping": in other words, you look for the jurisdiction that is the most favourable to the rights owner, and sue for infringement in that country. There can be marked differences between legal systems from one country to another: for instance, image rights are not part of the tradition of UK law, whereas other countries have established legal mechanisms for enforcing these rights.

In Spanish law, Beckham can take advantage of a "personality right" that allows him to protect himself against unauthorised commercial use of his name and image. Other countries have privacy, publicity or portrait rights that confer similar types of protection. Many US states have laws that grant notable individuals the exclusive right to exploit their image commercially. Article 9 of the French civil code recognises a similar right, as well as a right to privacy that can be used to prevent the commercialisation of one's image. And the German constitution grants individuals rights over how their appearance and name are used commercially.

A great example of forum shopping can be seen in the Oliver Kahn/EA Sports case recently settled in Germany. EA Sports is a producer of computer games; it used the name and likeness of Kahn, the goalkeeper for Bayern Munich and the German national team, in its highly successful FIFA World Cup 2002 computer game. EA insisted that it had obtained a licence from FIFPro, an international football players' union, that allowed it to use players' names and images. Kahn, however, argued that he had not *personally* given permission, and brought a successful action against EA Sports in a Hamburg court. EA was forced to withdraw all copies of its computer game from shelves across the whole of Germany.

If Beckham is to protect and maximise the revenues he makes from his brand, he will need the best possible advice on the complexities of the law and the new techniques that can be used for protective purposes. Sophisticated international brand management is vital. Couchman puts it like this:

> The skills required for developing a sports personality as a brand are generally beyond the capabilities of a traditional football agent. They are the skills of a modern branded company. Getting a good deal for a footballer is not about promoting a local hero who gets a boot deal, opens a few supermarkets and has a lifetime supply of Lucozade. The brand owners are very sophisticated, very strategic and commercially ruthless – pleasantly so, of course, they are not nasty people, they are just very good at the job of getting the best

deal for their companies. If you as a sports talent do not understand the language and mechanics of building brands, you will simply not know how to make the most money.

This is part of the reason for the increasing crossover between talent agencies and marketing and advertising agencies. The rights owner – in our case, the celebrity – has to understand the brand owner.

Beckham has demonstrated from an early stage in his career that he is good at getting the best advice on building his brand. He has also shown that he understands how important and how complex protecting his brand is, and has demonstrated that he will do what it takes to ward off any unfair and unauthorised attempts to make money from his image. In short, he has managed his brand exactly as any sensible, efficient branded business would be run.

There is one other aspect of protecting your brand that we need to look at: protecting its reputation. This is an important matter for any brand; allegations of tampering, unethical practices, illegal operations and the like could have disastrous consequences. And the more an allegation goes to the heart of what your brand is about, the more damaging it will be. Firestone never recovered from the allegations that faults in its tyres were responsible for deaths on the road; the Arthur Andersen brand was destroyed when its integrity was shattered by management malpractice.

Other brands that have bounced back have been able to do so because the core of their brand wasn't damaged, or because they had a bank of customer goodwill to draw on, or because their crisis management tactics were spot on. So Perrier weathered the benzene scandal because its brand was still well liked, and Tylenol survived a massive product recall after its product was deliberately contaminated with cyanide because it acted quickly and transparently, and in line with its values.

All brands face such crises; whether they sink or rise above them depends on how strong they are. Personality brands are particularly prone to these crises for the simple reason that they are people, with all the usual human flaws. Adultery, drug taking, lying, corruption and anti-social behaviour (getting drunk, swearing, fighting) are the most obvious examples of human fallibility that can affect the reputation of personality brands.

In April 2004, Beckham found his brand reputation under attack and his marriage under the microscope yet again following lurid allegations of adultery with more than one woman. The allegations, which first appeared in the British tabloid *News of the World*, seemed to have captivated the whole country. One observer described them as the biggest sex scandal since Princess Diana admitted she had been unfaithful to Prince Charles – not the first time that Posh and Becks have been compared to that royal couple. The international press was full of speculation that brand Beckham would be damaged and that sponsors would walk away from a man whose image had been tarnished.

At moments like this, a celebrity's spin machine goes into overdrive. Common tactics are:

1. Issuing a quick denial or near-denial
2. Having a short "wait and see" to find out how bad things are
3. Blackening the reputation of whoever is making the allegations
4. Finding a sympathetic angle for the press to cover
5. Offering an exclusive rebuttal
6. Threatening legal action or even issuing writs if things are getting really bad and you are innocent.

Beckham's spin machine acted quickly in the days following the allegations. The girl at the centre of the first claim had her entire sexual history publicised, and was accused of acting maliciously because she hadn't been offered a full-time job with Beckham's new management company. Meanwhile Becks made an emergency flight to France to be with Posh, offer his support and show how much in love they still were.

Still more claims came, and within a week there seemed to be hardly a girl in Madrid that Beckham hadn't been accused of bedding. The wildness of some of the allegations seemed to cast doubts on the credibility of the central accusation, and indeed that might have been the intention: to create a smokescreen around the first accusation to reduce its impact.

One interesting undercurrent in the coverage was the treatment meted out to Posh. There was an implication that she hadn't been a supportive wife, even a sentiment that "Well, you couldn't blame Becks after all Posh had put him through." This reflects views we have seen expressed before: that people don't warm so much to Posh as they do to Becks, and find her pushy where her husband is self-effacing. Rather like Princess Diana, Beckham seems to benefit from an "anti-spouse" factor. People made allowances for Diana's adultery because they liked her and could identify with her, whereas they didn't like Charles and found him stuck up. It is possible that people will find Beckham's indiscretion – if that's what it proves to be once the hysteria dies down – sympathetic, something that makes him a flawed but more believable character, a mere mortal, one of us. Indeed, if we look at the events of April 2004 in the context of Beckham's brand values, we may even be able to argue that they are capable of enhancing the brand.

First of all, let's consider Beckham's dedication. During the time of the alleged infidelities, he was leading England and establishing himself at Real Madrid, so the only question is whether the lack of dedication in his personal life will be seen as a one-off and forgivable lapse when put in the context of his continued dedication to his sport. To be sure, he and Victoria have made a concerted show of unity about their marriage and his devotion to her and the kids.

Second, there is Beckham's sense of style. This is largely irrelevant here, except in the sense that having beautiful girls claim you are a fabulous lover with immaculately groomed pubic hair attests to a certain popstar glamour.

Third, Beckham's down-to-earth humanity is not necessarily affected by the human failing of having perhaps been tempted to flirt or more with a beautiful girl. This could in fact make him more approachable and balance the New

Age squeaky-clean image projected by the man who meets Nelson Mandela, loves children and never says a bad word in public.

As this book goes to press, the brouhaha is still raging, but we can speculate about two scenarios for the Beckham brand.

It is often said that a brand that endures a crisis emerges stronger as a result. We have already seen Beckham put this theory into practice following his sending-off against Argentina. By acknowledging he was wrong and performing superbly over the next year, he bonded his audiences to him in a way he could never otherwise have done. In the current crisis, his values and his judgement are being called into question, but if he shows his customary dedication and down-to-earth approach in dealing with the consequences, he could emerge as a stronger person and more admired brand.

The second scenario stems from the concept that damage will be done to the Beckham brand only if its core product or values suffer. At the moment, the brand's success still depends on what happens on the football pitch. If Beckham fails to maintain his usual high standards, leads England to an early exit from Euro 2004, and gets dropped by Real Madrid, that will have a much greater impact on his marketability. Sponsors may be prepared to tolerate a penitent adulterer, but they can't be associated with a failure.

Worse still for Beckham, and what would certainly destroy his brand, would be if he were found to have knowingly taken performance-enhancing drugs, or to have cheated, or to have been bribed to throw a game. Acts like these would shatter his reputation and alienate everyone. Beckham's success on the pitch is still central to his brand. His best strategy for the next few years is to focus on his football.

Whatever happens, the adultery allegations provide living proof that managing a celebrity brand is uniquely difficult and that protecting its image is not just about technical issues of intellectual property or watertight contracts. Overseeing every area of a celebrity's private and public life requires a 24-hours-a-day, seven-days-a-week commitment. Indeed, it is probably the most demanding form of brand management there is.

Notes
1 "Public image limited," Nic Couchman, *Guardian*, 1 May 2002.

GOLDENBALL 8

Protecting your brand is not about firing off letters from lawyers; rather, it is a complex proactive process. The owner of legal rights has to understand the language of brand protection every bit as well as the traditional brand owner, and be every bit as aggressive.

THE FUTURE OF THE BRAND

Start planning your future now

"If you don't plan the future you want,
you get the one that turns up."

From **The Future of Brands**, edited by Rita Clifton and
Esther Maughan, Interbrand, Palgrave 1999

David Beckham will be 30 in 2005. How long can he go on making his living from soccer? Can he look forward to a future where he lives on in our hearts and minds as a great brand, but not as a footballer?

One of the great benefits of having a strong brand is that it provides some assurance that you will still be making money in the future. If people have come to know, trust and like you and have demonstrated their commitment by buying more of you year after year, then you can reasonably expect them to carry on doing so *if* (and it is a big if) you don't do anything to undermine their trust.

Moreover, this assurance of future earnings isn't confined to a brand's current range of products; future earnings from new activities are just as important. Brands endure long after the products they originally endorsed have died. Kodak is still big today, but who owns a Box Brownie? The company recently announced that it is to stop selling photographic film to concentrate on digital products.

But how does this work for celebrity or personality brands? Isn't there an inherent contradiction in the words of Sir Hector Laing if we think of people as brands? If a person dies, how can their brand endure?

Unlike branded companies, which may have thousands of employees and special structures in place to ensure there is a strong culture supporting the brand in good times and bad, the success or failure of a celebrity brand often rests on the shoulders of one person. In that sense, such brands can lack stability and longevity. The only celebrity brands that still command attention after many years are those of people like Bruce Springsteen, the Rolling Stones or Paul Newman – people who are still practising their craft, but who haven't developed the paraphernalia of merchandising and sponsorship deals in the same way as Beckham has.

However, this flaw in celebrity brands may disappear as the concept evolves and celebrities become more sophisticated and skilled at managing themselves as brands. A person may not live for long, but his or her beliefs, personality and image can live on and be passed down from one generation to another. Decades after their deaths, the images of Marilyn Monroe and James Dean continue to sell posters and T-shirts. If these celebrities can endure, surely any celebrity who is positive and proactive about managing their brand has a chance.

As a product, footballers have a short shelf-life. Once they hit 35 (if they even last that long) their playing days are likely to be over, and with them the commercial contracts that their fame pulled in. If Beckham keeps up his disciplined lifestyle and stays free of injury he may manage to stretch out his career for a little longer, but at some stage he will have to hang up his boots. What then?

In the old days, footballers were encouraged to learn a trade they could take up after they stopped playing. Many (including Alex Ferguson for a while) found running a pub the most convenient trade. On one level, Beckham's career as a fashion icon is merely a sophisticated update of the tradition of having something to do after your playing days are over.

It's fun to speculate about what will become of the Beckham brand after football. Here are some thoughts:

- The Beckham brand becomes a range of sports goods and eventually a branded sports experience store, and is ultimately floated on the stock market.
- Beckham runs his own fashion house with his own designs for clothes and interiors.
- Beckham goes to Hollywood, where his looks and estuary accent establish him as the new Michael Caine.
- Beckham concentrates on Asia and becomes a byword for all things chic and sporty there.
- Beckham turns to football management, taking Leyton Orient into the premiership, helping Manchester United acquire four successive European titles and leading England to win the FIFA World Cup
- Beckham becomes a roving goodwill ambassador. Together with his wife Victoria, he espouses the cause of the Tibetans and ensures that this small country preserves its independence from China.

Anything is possible, but what is probable?

To explore where the Beckham brand is likely to go in future, I talked to a range of brand experts from different areas of business and marketing. I asked them what they thought the Beckham brand stood for and where it might go after football. The rest of this chapter is given over to their speculations.

THE CUSTOMER EXPERIENCE GURU

Shaun Smith is a leading consultant advising companies worldwide on how to deliver a great customer experience that will build brand loyalty. He has worked with airlines, supermarkets and law firms. Here is his view:

The reason that David Beckham is successful as a brand is that he is much more than just a talented footballer. He projects what we call a brand experience. In other words, his fans perceive the totality of the Beckham brand through not only his on-pitch skills, but also his distinctive visual identity, his lifestyle and values, the products he chooses to endorse, his merchandise and books, and even the brands he buys himself: Gucci, Ferrari, and so on. Beckham represents a mosaic of associations and clues that together define him as a brand. The reason he has been so successful is that he realises this better than just about anyone else and has carefully managed all of these elements so that they tell a consistent and distinctive story: one that appeals to the aspirations and values of his target audience. Herein lies the challenge.

A few years ago, I was trekking in Nepal. We were climbing in an area high in the Himalayan snow-line several days from the nearest village. The porters, who were carrying our heavy equipment for a dollar or two a day, were clad in flip-flops and ragged T-shirts – except for one, that is. Proudly sporting a Manchester United shirt, this particular porter asked us at every rest stop about David Beckham. The moral of the story

Getty Images

is this: Beckham is now one of the most widely recognised icons in the world. He was mobbed in Japan by crowds of screaming schoolgirls who know next to nothing about football. His book *My Side* is the fastest-selling autobiography ever. In short, he is becoming ubiquitous, and when brands are everywhere they can begin to lose their cachet, their cool factor. Each new generation is looking for brands that define them and their values and that are in some way different to what has gone before. Brand fatigue is part of the problem that McDonald's is facing.

So does Beckham have to re-invent himself, rather like Madonna, in order to appeal to the new generation? As his football skills begin to fade, this will become increasingly difficult and so I think we are close to seeing the peak of

Beckham's fame as a footballer. As a new generation of fans emerge, so will a player with a new brand who will take over as the next football superstar.

However, as I started by saying, Beckham represents much more than just football and so it is easy to see how he could be successful in extending his brand into other areas while it is still fresh. An obvious example is sports or leisure wear, but given his interests, launching a fashion brand could leverage the strength of his name and image while enabling the brand to be updated to keep pace with new generations of consumers. But my advice, David, is do it soon and don't involve Victoria!

THE FOOTBALL MARKETERS

Juliet Slot is one of the new breed of professional marketers in football. A former Adidas executive, she is now marketing director for Fulham, one of the most ambitious clubs in the English Premier League. These are her thoughts:

David is one of the most successful personality brands in the world. What he has done incredibly well is allow his commercial associations to act as launch pads for more brand exposure while not undermining his core strengths. For example, Adidas: the performance sports athlete with fashion and style; Police: casual sunglasses presenting him as a fashion icon; Marks & Spencer: the family man developing affordable products for kids; Brylcreem: cool to wear again thanks to him.

I think in Asia he does not have the same people managing him, as I saw some dreadful associations, probably driven by Victoria's need to launch herself there when they went on tour last year. I thought they devalued him and looked like a cash-driven exercise, not a promotion of the Beckham brand.

I don't think he will make it in the US. What basis would he have, unless he was in the movies or played a US sport? If Victoria's music was more popular and she was more famous then maybe, but I don't see it happening.

If I were him I would already be developing soccer-related products that I could use to endorse and provide lifelong income: coaching programmes and books and videos building a "how I did it" image. I think he should base his future business in football and as an icon to kids. I don't think he will make a good manager, but then I don't think he will be allowed to be by his wife!

I think he will do TV presenting when he finishes; it would be great for him to do programmes for kids, for whom his inarticulacy is not a problem. They could be on Saturdays and would make soccer cool to both girls and boys, maybe fused with music (his other love) and fashion.

I don't think he will make Hollywood.

Peter Jones is a highly experienced marketer who has spent many years working with some of the best-known advertising and marketing firms in Europe. He is also deputy chairman of Plymouth Argyle, a Nationwide League club to which he has brought a marketer's business knowledge coupled with a fan's enthusiasm. In just over two years, he has helped transform the club into one of the most successful outside the premiership. He belongs to the group of future-watchers that sees the Beckham brand as transcending product categories:

When we set out to uncover the DNA of the Beckham brand, there's one question we need to resolve. Just how much is it exclusive to the individual, or to what degree is it built on the foundation of his relationship with his wife and children? In other words, are the key brand values to do with football, or with family? I believe the X factor is now more to do with the latter. It's about decency, humanity and a genuine love of children.

And that's where the opportunity lies. David Beckham is a universally appreciated role model. He has the chance, in partnership with Victoria, to generate some real impact on real lives in the real world, right across the globe.

He may well take the Eriksson/dell'Olio initiative – Truce International – as a model, and look to mould a Beckham equivalent in which he sets out to provide leadership and inspiration for countless millions of people to better their lives through the twin pillars he and Victoria know best: sport and music.

THE INTERNATIONAL BRAND CONSULTANT

Terry Oliver is the Asia-Pacific CEO of Interbrand, the world's longest-established brand management consultancy. Based in Tokyo, he witnessed the Beckham brand's impact on Asia at first hand:

Since his appearance in the 2002 World Cup, David Beckham has been riding a wave of popularity here. His success as a highly-paid celebrity in markets around the world transcends the soccer pitch. In Japan, Beckham's face is ubiquitous. He has become a recognisable celebrity endorser of foods, fragrances and cellphones, to name just a few. But can his brand survive over time the way strong brands do?

Many marketing specialists feel Beckham will maintain his popularity providing he reinforces it through continued success on the soccer field and in image management, fashion leadership and business licensing. But for his brand to sustain its appeal and stay in the public eye, he requires skilled professional management. Can he continue on this path after he retires from the game and his youthful good looks fade?

While some sports heroes have remained icons for decades, their popularity is usually based on their appeal to compatriots or partisans. Even a legendary star like Michael Jordan seems to be passing from the scene because of poor brand management.

Another wild card is the fickle nature of today's Japanese consumers. The culture has a voracious appetite for foreign faces and fads, but is constantly looking for something new. That's why I believe the most likely scenario is that the Beckham brand will fade after a few years in the limelight. The truth is that Beckham is far from being a truly great soccer player. While he won't disappear altogether, he will most likely retire to sports category advertising and promotions, which is, after all, where he plays best.

THE SPORTS MARKETING LAWYER

Nic Couchman is a founder of Couchman Harrington, a leading sports law practice. He has advised many sports personalities, clubs and leagues on how to protect and enhance the value of their intellectual property, and especially their brands.

The future for Beckham will probably be as a product endorsement for sports products. However, there are risks to this: the longer Beckham is retired from the game, the less relevant his appeal will be. One of the most interesting scenarios for him is if he can make it into America. That is why the Real Madrid deal is so important. If he can excel for them and make himself a real hero, he will win a place in the hearts of millions of Hispanics around the world, including in America. He could then use his niche appeal to this group to establish himself in America.

THE US PERSPECTIVE

Chuck Brymer is the worldwide CEO of the Interbrand group, based in New York. He has a sobering perspective on the Beckham brand's appeal in the States:

The so-called arrival of soccer in the US has been met with far less fanfare than was originally thought, at least at the professional level. Sure, there are countless soccer moms with SUVs filled with young schoolchildren going to soccer practice, but the interest of these kids soon starts to fade as they become older and begin watching and playing the big three: baseball, basketball and American football. I guess that major league [professional] soccer is up and running in the US, but I'm damned if I know of any teams or stars that play it. My guess is that I am far from alone.

Beckham is known here now after his press tour a few months back. But he is still not on the level of A-list celebrities or other well-known athletes (Shaquille, Tiger, and so on). Nor do I think he will be as long as soccer fails to generate a mass audience. I suppose if he played here instead of Real Madrid, he might be able to raise awareness of the game. More than likely, though, he would be known more for simply being a celebrity athlete than a soccer player. Kind of like Paris Hilton: she is a celebrity, but no one has an idea why.

My guess is that soccer will be a sport that Americans eventually begin to watch every four years when their team (which is getting better) plays in the World Cup. This is much like swimming, gymnastics, track and other sports, which we watch every four years during the Olympics because of national pride rather than the game itself. To many, it is not a good television sport; it's too slow and not enough points are scored. It's like baseball, which doesn't get a good TV audience until the playoffs.

So if soccer remains as limited in its appeal as I believe it will, and David Beckham's core appeal comes from being a soccer player, I can't see how he can ever really make it big out here.

THE EUROPEAN VIEW

Tom Blackett is one of the most respected brand consultants in Europe, and has been named as one of the 50 most influential people in the automotive industry, where he has helped create brand names for some of the biggest car makers. He is equally sceptical about Beckham's chances of making it big in the States, but sees Europe as an option.

David Beckham is famous for three things: his skills as a footballer, his wife and his taste in clothes. Could he make it big in the US? Well, they're not really into soccer, they have little idea who his wife is and they've got plenty of glamorous walking clotheshorses of their own. He could – just *could* – make a minor splash in the latter role, but it would be fleeting.

But as far as Europe or elsewhere in the soccer-mad world is concerned, things could be different. Italy is his natural home. There they worship football, good looks and fashion;

he and Posh have all the necessary attributes. I can see him setting up a football academy in conjunction with Prada, or the two of them [David and Victoria] establishing their own fashion house. I'm sure they'd both love it there (perhaps that's why they called the nipper Romeo) – unless the siren call of Essex is too strong.

THE WRITER

One of the top writers in the world of business, John Simmons has written best-selling books on how to communicate brands to people in a creative and distinctive way. Despite being an Arsenal supporter, he knows a bit about football, but he knows a lot more about brands.

The obvious thought is that Beckham will outlive his football career through own-brand clothing. He's made steps into this area, and as he grows older he can become, like Giorgio Armani, stylishly older. But I think of the failure of Bjorn Borg underwear, for example, and I'm not sure if this will be the long-term route for Beckham.

I think David Beckham could become the new Princess Di. He will develop his communication skills (they're coming along anyway), adding to his innate ability to project empathy with the young, vulnerable and disadvantaged. As he does this, he will gather good causes around him in all parts of the world. He will be appointed a United Nations global ambassador, bringing a sense of hope to despairing regions of the world. When Nigeria becomes the first African country to win the World Cup in 2014, beating China in the final, both countries will dedicate their success to David Beckham.

This provides the Beckham brand with a power, almost a sanctity, above the usual kinds of own-branding or product endorsement. He will not need to sell any of his own products; David Beckham sportswear might not be the best, particularly when he's no longer on the pitch. So the Beckham brand will deliver most commercial value through carefully selected brand associations. The world's biggest consumer brands will want to be seen in relationship with the Beckham brand as a way of enhancing and softening their own image.

In effect, Beckham becomes a kind of Spice Boy, adding flavour to big brands that have started to seem a bit bland. And one of those brands will be a global charity dedicated to the elimination of poverty and the cause of peace.

THE NEW COMMUNICATIONS SPECIALISTS

Ben Wells and Adrian New are highly experienced consultants with Redmandarin, a company that specialises in helping businesses take advantage of new technologies and forms of communication to build their brands. Ben Wells is based in London.

I see him as being more of a lifestyle than a football icon after he retires. His agency, 19, talks about the Beckham brand, but I think there is a clash between the values he brings and those of his wife. He is dedicated as a player, husband and father; he is stylish, talented and hard-working. She unfortunately can appear to some people as self-centred, egotistical, talentless and a little plastic. In other words, whatever brand they are looking to exploit, she may be a hindrance.

The reality of his commercial situation is that he has about 10 or 12 commercial partners and I think wouldn't countenance investments of anything less than £1 million per year. Clearly this is going to cut out a number of potentially interested parties, but as he gets nearer retirement, I'd guess he'll need to reappraise this. Real Madrid owns 50 percent of his commercial rights [on new deals], and most contracts he has will terminate when he is in his early 30s. I can't see too many brands rushing to buy a piece of Beckham at those costs thereafter.

Beckham-named merchandise accounted for a large proportion of official MUFC sales, but I would argue that playing for United was the making of him; the fact that he is a talented (if limited) player with good looks just added to the package. I don't think we'd be talking today about the Beckham brand if he had come through the youth system at Arsenal, for example.

I can't see him being taken seriously as a manager or a media pundit after he retires, and let's be honest, his looks are going to fade as he gets older and he'll be usurped before long as the face of brands X, Y and Z by younger, hipper models. I am also dubious of the track record of 19 in marketing non-music clients, and think they will have to push him away from the football route simply because they won't understand it.

All in all the brand may last for another five years, with limited interest in the UK, Spain (while he's at Madrid) and the Far East, but I think it will be irrelevant to most people once he stops playing. His market will move from men (Vodafone, Police sunglasses, Brylcreem) to women as people exploit his looks rather than his footballing ability to sell products. I would guess also that after five years or so, 19 will have made its money and be looking for the next novelty act to impose on the unsuspecting public.

Adrian New is based in Asia, and has a different perspective:

Beckham will be the next Princess Di when he retires from footy. He won't go into management, but will adopt some kind of goodwill ambassador role either for the UK or for the UN, probably incorporating children. His appeal crosses sexes: guys want to be him and women just love him. He also crosses ages. Virtually the only role models for post-30 males today are film stars, and Beckham can provide a model, in every sense, for the generation that has grown up with him. Any fashion brands targeting that sector will continue to use him, although he'll probably want to continue to develop his own brand and designs. I don't see his image becoming tarnished or outdated; he's too smart for that. His brand values stretch way beyond football, encompassing honesty, integrity, family virtues and hard work. The goodwill he has built up will continue in football for at least another four years, and I think he'll become even more valuable when he retires. There is no one else in the Western world that comes close to his popularity in the East, and that will be crucial for many brands looking to create a market position in the key markets of Japan and China. His move to Madrid has already shown that his brand is stronger than that of Man Utd. There were no Real Madrid shirts to be seen in Singapore a year ago; now they are everywhere.

THE ADVERTISING SPECIALIST

Gwyn Jones is the managing director of Bartle Bogle Hegarty, one of the most respected and influential advertising agencies in Europe and Asia. He has advised some of the biggest brand names in the world on how to build their image, including Levi's. I have given him the last word because his views are closest to my own:

Unlike many other celebrity brands, Beckham isn't just a confection of image and fame but is rooted in fantastic core product delivery. He is a great player who works hard at his game. The move to Madrid, I would argue, is a classic example of great brand management. This was not a marketing- or image-driven move, but a way for him to innovate and improve the actual product performance, and in so doing develop the status of the brand.

While the Beckham brand is tied to his performances on the pitch and those performances are great – the stuff of comic-book heroism in fact – then everything looks good. The clothes, the hair, the wife, all add up to a great brand package.

When we consider life beyond the playing career, things get more interesting. Does he just exploit his cumulative brand status and lend his name to everything from hair gel to underwear, or does he need to find a new avenue for core product delivery? For my money, he will be better off if he continues to *do* something, not just *be* something. That something should, like football, be something he is both good at and passionate about, and probably something to do with kids: sport, education, even health care. The Beckham Foundation – why not? If the Beckhams are the new royalty, maybe he needs his own Prince's Trust.

MY VIEW

I think Gwyn is largely right – not that there are really any rights or wrongs here. The Beckham brand has achieved what it has so far because it has *done* something, not just been something. And it is something he can genuinely care about. Beckham has repeatedly revealed his soft side and shown how important public displays of love are to him. He has shown interest in and comfort with the lifestyles and views of many different people, from meeting Nelson Mandela to revelling in his role as a gay icon. What ties it all together is paradoxically his down-to-earth humanity.

However, we have to accept that Beckham is human, and that people are flawed and often fail to live up to the high ideals they set themselves or are set by others. The Beckham brand will be tested many times over the next few years.

Getty Images

David Beckham may face more allegations because of who he is and the position he holds.

Nevertheless, I think Beckham still has the potential to be a great role model, a wonderful roving ambassador for good causes. This wouldn't stop him exploiting his brand name for commercial purposes; indeed, it would provide people with a real reason to buy his products. So I still see him putting his name to sports products and fashion items, but on top of that, leveraging the goodwill he has created and sharing the profits with his own foundation. It could use football as a tool to help children grow, learn and enjoy life.

Whatever he does, he needs to start thinking about it quickly. Time is no friend to any brand manager, and it certainly isn't on the side of any footballer.

GOLDENBALL 9

Having a strong brand gives you options to develop in the future, but you need to think quickly, plan carefully and move as swiftly as you can while you have the advantage of a lot of goodwill. You cannot live on your reputation for very long.

10
GOLDENBALLS

Nine rules to play the game and win

So what have we learnt about the brand of the man whom his wife affectionately calls "Goldenballs"?

Beckham is a unique brand, but one that demonstrates the well-established principles and time-honoured processes for managing any brand. His product is strong, with complementary values and a personality that transcends it, so allowing him to enter new markets and countries. He lives his values and delivers his promise to consumers. He has a complex brand identity that enables him to find new ways of commercialising his brand while staying true to the same basic look.

He is commercially smart and thus highly profitable and valuable. He has chosen his co-branding partners with care and has benefited from each of them. He has been ruthless about protecting his brand. Finally, like any great brand, the Beckham brand has enormous possibilities still before it.

Here, for convenience, is a summary of those goldenballs from each chapter.

Goldenball 1 To be a great brand, you have to have a great product in the first place: not necessarily a better product, but something that is different, that you are dedicated to and that you constantly strive to improve. Brands are like footballers in this respect: play off your past and you will soon be out of the team.

Goldenball 2 Managing a brand is a systematic process covering a multiplicity of factors. Celebrities are no longer just endorsers of other people's products; they are brands in their own right, and are learning how to manage themselves as such.

Goldenball 3 Brands are built on core values that people admire, and are communicated through a personality that people like. Celebrity brands are just the same; they have to be clear about their purpose and values, and act accordingly.

Goldenball 4 A celebrity manages his or her identity with the same meticulous attention to detail and awareness of its impact as a typical brand. Every look, every syllable of your name, every stitch of your clothes and every follicle of your hair is part of your brand identity and needs to be treated with care.

Goldenball 5 The best brands set out to do what they say. So it is with personalities as brands. Have a clear goal, stay true to yourself and make sure you get the maximum amount of credit for what you have done.

Goldenball 6 Commercialising a personality brand requires you to think not only about how much you can earn right now, but also about how any deal is going to help you achieve your brand goals and sustain your revenues in the long term.

Goldenball 7 Managing relationships with clubs, other celebrities and even national teams is all part of brand building. You have to choose your partners with care, and manage them with even more care.

Goldenball 8 Protecting your brand is not about firing off letters from lawyers; rather, it is a complex proactive process. The owner of legal rights has to understand the language of brand protection every bit as well as the traditional brand owner, and be every bit as aggressive.

Goldenball 9 Having a strong brand gives you options to develop in the future, but you need to think quickly, plan carefully and move as swiftly as you can while you have the advantage of a lot of goodwill. You cannot live on your reputation for very long.

Russel Wong Photography

MILESTONES IN THE DEVELOPMENT OF THE BECKHAM BRAND

Career highlights

1991   Signs as trainee for Manchester United
Appoints Tony Stephens as agent

1992   Wins FA Youth Cup
Makes senior team debut with Man Utd in Coca-Cola Cup

1993   Signs as professional for Man Utd

1994   Makes first full starting appearance against Galatasaray

1995   Makes league debut for Man Utd against Leeds

1996   Scores 60-yard lob over Wimbledon keeper Neil Sullivan from inside own half in the opening league game of the season
Makes international debut for England against Moldova
Sky Sports/Panasonic Young Player award
Sky Sports/Panasonic Fans' Footballer award

1997   PFA Young Player of the Year
Ranked 2nd in PFA Player of the Year

1998   Sent off in England v. Argentina match, 2nd round of 1998 World Cup

1999   Played a vital role in Man Utd treble winning run
First child, Brooklyn Beckham, born in March
Married Victoria Adams in July
Ranked 2nd in European Player of the Year

2000   Ranked 2nd in FIFA World Footballer of the Year
Ranked 2nd in BBC Sports Personality of the Year
Appointed captain of England team
Publishes his autobiography, *My World*

2001   Sports Writers' Association Sportsman of the Year
BBC Sports Personality of the Year
Ranked 2nd in FIFA World Player of the Year
Britain's Sportsman of the Year
Led England to World Cup Finals 2002 with a sterling performance in final qualifier against Greece

2002   Captained England to a quarter-final berth in World Cup 2002

2003   Well-publicised fallout with Alex Ferguson
Signs for Real Madrid for £25 million
Awarded OBE for efforts on and off the football pitch

Commercial highlights

1997   Signs a deal with Brylcreem for £1 million to promote its haircare products

Signs a deal with Pepsi to promote its drinks as part of Team Pepsi*

First deal with Adidas

2001   Signs a 3-year deal with Rage Software for £1.5 million a year to star in football computer games

Signs a £1 million deal with Italian eyewear designer Police sunglasses to become its UK face

2002   First solo male on cover of *Marie Claire*

Signs 3-year deal with Marks & Spencer for £3 million a year to promote DB07 range of children's clothing

Signs a deal with Vodafone for £1 million a year to star in TV ads and allow his voice to be used for a mobile phone mailbox service

Signs a 2-year deal with Castrol for £500,000 a year to promote its petroleum products

2003   Appoints Simon Fuller to manage and develop the Beckham brand

Appoints Terry Byrne, Watford's director of football, as his personal manager

Signs an estimated £2.2 million deal to promote Tokyo Beauty Centre beauty salons in Japan

Signs a £2.5 million deal to promote Meiji chocolate confectionery in Japan

2004   Ends relationship with Tony Stephens

Brings out new logo based on his distinctive style of free kick

Reportedly clinches a £40 million deal to become the new worldwide face of Gillette

* Exact date of deal not confirmed, but it falls between mid-1997, when Pepsi first got involved in football sponsorship, and mid-1998, when Beckham began endorsing its products.

EPILOGUE: THE GOLDEN BALLS-UP?

So what will happen now that David Beckham has allegedly confessed to his sexual indiscretions? Is he guilty of a monumental error of judgement that will tarnish his reputation and damage his standing with the public and his sponsors? Or will he emerge from the episode stronger than ever?

As I have said before, the great brands survive the toughest crises. Indeed, if they respond to these crises in the right way, they can actually deepen consumers' commitment. But it takes time to see what the impact of a crisis may be. Another chapter is waiting to be written in the story of Brand Beckham.

BIBLIOGRAPHY

David Beckham, *My Side* (HarperCollins, London, 2003)

David Beckham, *My World* (Hodder & Stoughton, London, 2000)

Abraham H. Maslow, *Toward a Psychology of Being* (John Wiley & Sons, New York, 1998)

Andy Milligan and Shaun Smith (eds), *Uncommon Practice: People who deliver a great brand experience* (FT Prentice Hall, London, 2002)

Irving Rein, Philip Kotler and Martin Stoller, *High Visibility: The making and marketing of professionals into celebrities* (NTC Business Books, Lincolnwood, Ill, 1997)

Ronald M. Shapiro and Mark A. Jankowski, *The Power of Nice: How to negotiate so everyone wins – especially you!* (John Wiley & Sons, New York, 2001)

CONTACTS

If you wish to find out about some of the companies and organisations that have been mentioned in this book, these websites offer more details:

Consultancy
Peter Jones
organic.eu@btconnect.com

Sponsorship and new media
Redmandarin
www.redmandarin.com

Brand consultancy
Interbrand
www.interbrand.com

Sports and image rights law
Couchman Harrington Associates
www.chass.co.uk

Customer service and customer experience consultancy
Shaun Smith
www.shaunsmithco.com

Advertising
Bartle Bogle Hegarty
www.bbh.co.uk

GUINNESS IS GUINNESS ...
THE COLOURFUL STORY OF A BLACK AND WHITE BRAND
MARK GRIFFITHS

People say "Guinness is Guinness", but it's not as black and white as that. When you pick up that monochrome pint, you're about to taste 250 colourful years of global heritage whose ingredients are astounding innovation, obsessive quality, memorable advertising and a passionate devotion to remaining the world's top stout.

Guinness is Guinness ... tells the story of a truly global brand that's more than just a beer. Today, Guinness is accepted everywhere it trades because it employs local people, uses local resources, adapts to local tastes, advertises with local relevance and reverence *as well as* giving people a product they can enjoy and relax with. All are factors that combine to give a modern meaning to the 75-year old gone-but-not-forgotten advertising slogan, "Guinness is good for you." Does it really taste better in Ireland, its spiritual home? For those who want to get to the bottom of the glass, this book of stories reveals the answer to this and provides fascinating insights into a brand that has inspired warmth in drinkers and non-drinkers alike for a quarter of a millennium.

> *"Whether writing about beer or bubble bath, Mark will get under the skin of a brand in order to expose the truth. He'll make you smile one minute and be in your face the next. Writing like that gets my vote every time."*
>
> **DAME ANITA RODDICK, FOUNDER, THE BODY SHOP**

If you're interested in Guinness; if you want to learn lessons from one great brand to shine a light on another; if you want to read a good story ... read on.

MY SISTER'S A BARISTA
HOW THEY MADE STARBUCKS
A HOME FROM HOME
JOHN SIMMONS

Coffee is a commodity. You can get a cup at any café, sandwich bar or restaurant anywhere. So how did Starbucks manage to reinvent coffee as a whole new experience, and create a hugely successful brand in the process?

My sister's a barista tells the Starbucks story from its origins in a Seattle fish market to its growing global presence today. This is a story that has un-folded quickly – at least in terms of conventional business

"Sit down with a cup of coffee, put your feet up, and be prepared to be riveted by the story of Starbucks. A fascinating read, by a fascinating writer."

RITA CLIFTON, CHAIRMAN, INTERBRAND

development. Starbucks is a phenomenon. Unknown 15 years ago, it now ranks among the 100 most valuable brands in the world. It has become the quintessential brand of the modern age, built around the creation of an experience that can be consistently reproduced across the world.

In exploring the secrets behind Starbucks' success, this book also tackles the wider question of what makes a successful brand. But ultimately it is a fascinating human story to inspire all of us.